THICKER THAN BLOOD

THICKER THAN BLOOD
Bonds of Fantasy and Reality in Adoption

edited by
Salman Akhtar, m.d.,
and Selma Kramer, m.d.

JASON ARONSON INC.
Northvale, New Jersey
London

This book was set in 12 pt. Bembo by Alabama Book Composition of Deatsville, Alabama, and printed and bound by Book-mart Press, Inc. of North Bergen, NJ.

Copyright © 2000 by Jason Aronson Inc.

10 9 8 7 6 5 4 3 2 1

Library of Congress Cataloging-in-Publication Data

Thicker than blood : bonds of fantasy and reality in adoption / edited by Salman Akhtar, Selma Kramer.
    p. cm.
    Includes bibliographical references and index.
    ISBN 0-7657-0266-5
    1. Adoption—Psychological aspects. 2. Separation-individuation. 3. Attachment behavior. I. Akhtar, Salman, 1946 July 31- II. Kramer, Selma.
    HV875.T53 2000
    362.73'4—dc21
                                                    00-020263

Printed in the United States of America on acid-free paper. For information and catalog write to Jason Aronson Inc., 230 Livingston Street, Northvale, NJ 07647-1726, or visit our website: www.aronson.com

To the memory

of Margaret S. Mahler—

teacher, friend, source of inspiration

Contents

10
Toward Optimizing the
Adopted Child's Development   **211**
Concluding Reflections
Robert C. Prall, M.D. and Henri Parens, M.D.

Acknowledgment

Chapters 2, 3, 6, 7, 8, and 9 were originally presented as papers at the 30th Annual Margaret S. Mahler Symposium on Child Development held on May 1, 1999, in Philadelphia. First and foremost, therefore, we wish to express our gratitude to the Margaret S. Mahler Psychiatric Research Foundation. We are also grateful to Michael Vergare, M.D., Chairman of the Department of Psychiatry and Human Behavior at Jefferson Medical College, as well as to the Philadelphia Psychoanalytic Institute and Society for their shared sponsorship of the symposium. Many colleagues from the Institute and Society helped during the symposium, and we remain grateful to them. Finally, we wish to acknowledge our sincere appreciation of Maryann Nevin for her efficient organization of and assistance during the symposium, and her outstanding skills in the preparation of this book's manuscript.

Contributors

Salman Akhtar, M.D.
Professor of Psychiatry, Jefferson Medical College; Training and
Supervising Analyst, Philadelphia Psychoanalytic Institute

Jennifer M. Bonovitz, Ph.D.
Faculty, Philadelphia Psychoanalytic Institute and Institute of
the Philadelphia Society for Clinical Social Work; Co-chair,
South Asia Forum of the Philadelphia Psychoanalytic Institute
and Society

Ira Brenner, M.D.
Clinical Associate Professor of Psychiatry, Jefferson Medical College; Training and Supervising Analyst, Philadelphia Psychoanalytic Institute

M. Hossein Etezady, M.D.
Clinical Director of Psychiatric Services, Paoli Memorial Hospital;
Faculty, Philadelphia Psychoanalytic Institute

Elaine Frank, M.S.W.
Co-Director, After Adoption and Parenting Services for Families, Philadelphia; former faculty and staff member of Infant Psychiatry Program, Medical College of Pennsylvania/Eastern Pennsylvania Psychiatric Institute

Selma Kramer, M.D.
Professor of Psychiatry, Jefferson Medical College; Training and Supervising Analyst, Philadelphia Psychoanalytic Institute

Carlotta G. Miles, M.D.
Faculty, Extension Division, Washington Psychoanalytic Institute; Psychiatric Consultant, The Johns Hopkins School of International Studies, The National Cathedral School for Girls, and The Madeira School; Practice of adult psychoanalysis and adult and child psychiatry

Henri Parens, M.D.
Professor of Psychiatry, Jefferson Medical College; Training and Supervising Analyst, Philadelphia Psychoanalytic Institute

Robert C. Prall, M.D.
Child, adolescent, and adult Psychoanalyst; Visiting Professor of Child Psychiatry, Medical College of Pennsylvania

Katherine Reed, M.D.
Clinical Assistant Professor of Psychiatry, University of Pennsylvania; Program Chair and Faculty, Philadelphia Psychoanalytic Institute

Denise Rowe, B.A.
Co-Director, After Adoption and Parenting Services for Families, Philadelphia; former faculty and staff member of Infant Psychiatry Program, Medical College of Pennsylvania/Eastern Pennsylvania Psychiatric Institute

Marshall D. Schechter, M.D.

Professor Emeritus of Child and Adolescent Psychiatry, University of Pennsylvania; Philadelphia Psychoanalytic Institute

Martin A. Silverman, M.D.

Clinical Professor of Psychiatry and Former Chair, Child Analysis Section, New York University College of Medicine; Training and Supervising Analyst and Supervising Child Analyst, New York University Psychoanalytic Institute; Training and Supervising Analyst, New York Psychoanalytic Institute; Associate Editor, *The Psychoanalytic Quarterly*

Paul R. Viola, M.D.

Faculty of Child and Adult Program of the Philadelphia Psychoanalytic Institute; Teaching Faculty of Psychotherapy Training Program of the Philadelphia Psychoanalytic Institute

1

THE MULTIFACETED PSYCHOSOCIAL IMPACT OF ADOPTION

M. Hossein Etezady, M.D.
Salman Akhtar, M.D.
and Selma Kramer, M.D.

Adoption is a complex psychosocial process. The emotionally charged transaction profoundly affects all the parties involved. Its impact, while variable, depending on each individual's role, is often multifaceted and can be everlasting. The biological parents of the child have to confront and master puzzling and contradictory emotions. On the one hand, they might feel a sense of relief at having given up the baby for adoption. Not infrequently, such babies are conceived under difficult circumstances and their parents are psychophysically ill-equipped to take care of them. On the other hand, the parents, especially the biological mother, are also riddled with feelings of loss, wistfulness, and guilt. There might also remain a lifelong desire to undo the act of having given up the child to someone else.

The adoptive parents face their own dilemmas. On the one hand, they enjoy the developmental pleasure of having a baby, a pleasure that is more marked if they have not had their own biological children. They might take conscious or unconscious pride in the generous aspect of their act while simultaneously reaping the psychic rewards of having realized an unconscious "family romance" (Freud 1908) fantasy. On the other hand, raising an adopted child might also increase the ambivalence that is normally felt in child rearing; this might burden the parents' ego. The "ordinary parental aggression" (Kramer 1995, p. 4) toward children might be heightened under such circumstances, causing anxiety to the adoptive parents.

The adopted children also have to negotiate much ambivalence. On the one hand, they might be aware that life has given them a second chance, that things are perhaps better in their adoptive home than they might have been in the home of their biological parents, and that they are receiving the benefits of parents who want them and are willing to undergo the usual (and sometimes unusual) sacrifices to raise them well. On the other hand, their sense of belonging to their (adoptive) parents might remain shaky and in need of greater than ordinary "emotional refueling" (Mahler et al. 1975). They might also worry about their origins and the reasons for their having been given away by their biological parents; a sense of secret inferiority might develop around such a nidus of worry.

If there are any preexisting siblings in the family, they, too, are affected by the arrival of an adopted child. The biological children of the adoptive parents feel both an internal sense of privilege as well as unconscious guilt in the face of such secret entitlement. Moreover, a child's learning about the adoption of a sibling stirs up an uncertainty in his mind "not only about the circumstances of that sibling's birth, but about his own origin as well" (Jacobs 1988, p. 33). The effect of adoption, however, extends beyond the familial orbit and involves acquaintances and even the society at large. Adoption invariably evokes mixed emotions in friends, neighbors, and acquaintances. On the one hand, there is a sense of respect and admiration for the courage and generosity of the adoptive parents. On the other hand, fantasies of all kind get projected upon them; the adoptive parents and the adopted children unwittingly become "containers" (Bion 1967) of unmetabolized sexual, aggressive, and family romance fantasies of the larger group surrounding them.

Thus, issues of profound ambivalence are involved in adoption, and such ambivalence crops up in a variety of situations involving adoption. We will address each of these individual areas in some depth, highlighting the dilemmas specific to them, with the hope that such knowledge will lead to deeper understanding of the ambivalence.

IMPACT ON THE BIOLOGICAL PARENTS

Although many circumstances may determine the need for parents to give up their biological child for adoption, one common situation involves a young woman who has conceived her child in undesirable circumstances: the pregnancy is seldom intended or wanted. The putative father is frequently a transient figure in the woman's life. The young woman is perhaps an object of seduction, abuse, rape, or other indignities. The discovery of the pregnancy is unwelcome news, and for the most part it is the opening salvo in a series of explosive and unsettling critical events. Guilt, shame, denial and confusion, depression, remorse, helplessness and self-loathing, and episodes of running away, suicidal, or other self-destructive behavior are nearly universal and beset the unhappy woman for a long time. Negative reactions from her family and friends are typical. The decision to give up the child for adoption is not reached without considerable agony and mental anguish. The young woman, still suffering from the trauma of her ill-fated sexual liaison, now has to come to grips with the unthinkable catastrophe of having conceived an illegitimate child. Her options are few and unpleasant. The family resources, finances, and emotional capacities are usually in short supply and she cannot rely on help or relief from the putative father. Adoption is presented to her as the only acceptable alternative to suicide or abortion.

This tragic picture is in stark contrast to that of the legitimate birth that serves to complete and solidify the identity of a young woman as an independent adult, happily nestled in the secure comfort and harmony of her marital relationship. In the latter situation, the woman's marriage was the realization of hopes and fondest wishes of herself and her husband as well of those of many well-wishing relatives and friends. The pregnancy was most likely planned, wanted, and anticipated with great joy and idealized expectations. When the marriage and its circumstances are optimal, the pregnancy deepens and enriches the intimate and interdependent reliance of the couple on one another. It enhances the self-esteem and the sense of well-being of the expectant couple. It brings the future and its many promises of fulfillment and joy into a sharp and well-delineated focus. The birth of the child is greeted with an outpouring of emotional intensity and triumphant celebration that engulfs the couple and the circle of their family and friends. This momentous event, more than any other, seals and forever underlies the core identity of the new parents as individuals, the couple as members of a family unit, and the family as an integral part of the community. The parents' lives are never the same again, as the well-being and the requirements of their offspring take precedence over much that had once been the focus of their undivided devotion and full attention. Their joint hopes and aspirations for their baby strengthen their bond and solidify their union. Sometimes a stagnant relationship is rejuvenated and a faltering union is repaired and revitalized.

In contrast, a young woman with an illegitimate pregnancy is alone, and must deal with uncontrollable events fraught with pain, isolation, and fear. Once the ordeal of pregnancy and then the frightening prospect of giving birth are behind her, she has to come to grips with the proposition of giving away her newborn, which, by the immutable dictates of biology and instinct, is now an essential component of her emotional being. Here scenarios vary. Almost all these mothers receive some degree of help, be it financial or moral support, from ambivalent and resentful family members, from charitable organizations, or from religious institutions. Some biological mothers never recover from this traumatic loss of their baby, which dominates and disturbs all subsequent milestones of their lives. Others, more fortunate and endowed with uncommon resiliency, may in time and perhaps with treatment heal enough to live a relatively productive and manageable life. Perhaps the most fortunate of these scenarios is that which is commonly known as "open adoption." Here the adoptive parents in essence nurture, support, and protect the biological mother. After the adoptive parents take the child, the biological mother maintains access to the baby. This downgrades the trauma endured by the mother from the nearly unbearable loss to the more common anguish of separation.

Women who have given up their children for adoption never recover from their sense of loss, guilt, and mourning. They search for their babies for years to follow. They have elaborate fantasies about the children's fate and life circumstances. They look for them in crowds, in other cities, and in unfamiliar places. Every time someone is reported lost or killed, but is not identified, they seek information that might dispel their fear that the victim could be their lost child. Some eventually meet their child after years of wishing, hoping, and incessantly planning. But all the while they are haunted by the impact of their tragic experience and beleaguered by shame, guilt, and self-loathing as they idealize their lost child.

IMPACT ON THE ADOPTIVE PARENTS

By the time the adoption of a child is completed, the adoptive parents have been through a long series of emotional upheavals with a happy ending that is actually the beginning rather than the end. The responsibilities of raising a child, with its many rewards and unexpected pains and disappointments, still lie ahead. Adoptive parents have had to come to terms with the recognition of the fact that one of their most cherished ambitions, namely the developmental achievements of bearing their own offspring, is not to come to fruition. This is a massive disappointment that sorely tests the brittle equilibrium of a young couple's mental resilience in individual terms and in the matrix of their marital relationship. Disappointment, rage, and grief, as well as denial, projection, and displacement in various forms, precede the resolution and acceptance of this unhappy fate. When the couple, together as a unit and individually, can weather this storm they come to see adoption as their only remaining hope. However, they do not reach this point of resignation or resolution until they have gone through years of medical and gynecological consultations, psychological counseling, and fertility procedures; their hope is gone, and many thousands of dollars have been spent.

Adoption is initially seen as the least desired option, the last resort to be utilized only when all other measures have been thoroughly exhausted. The source of the adopted child and the legal, bureaucratic, and geographical obstacles that have to be overcome vary greatly from case to case. These variables play a part in determining the affective experience, fantasy, and expectations of the adoptive parents in relationship to their own self view, their parental identity, and their attitude toward their mate. More important, this process has a major impact on the baby and its future. This impact is similar to the impact that the events and the course and quality of the parental experience during pregnancy have on natural parents' relationship to their newborn and on the quality of the child's attachment. In adoption, as in the natural birth of a child, bonding and attachment for parents are complex and delicate by-products of their past experiences, their psychological makeup, and their fantasies and expectations, and of the biological endowment, physical characteristics, and particular temperament of the child. Moreover, the adoptive parents (especially the mother) have to free themselves internally from their own tendency to devalue their adoptive parenthood in order to enjoy caring for their adopted offspring (Helene Deutsch, quoted in Schechter 1967).

When there is a suitable fit and a fortunate match between the parents and the child, subsequent development tends to be far more favorable. A mismatch or absence of a suitable fit complicates subsequent steps and may significantly interfere with parental empathy and the child's capability to make appropriate use of the parents' available resources in his or her rudimentary self-organization. Parents with greater innate capacity for empathy and reflective function have a better chance of handling a mismatch. When the events preceding the birth of the biological offspring or before the acquisition of an adopted child have resulted in depletion or destabilization of emotional resources of the prospective parent, empathic attunement and reflective capacity are compromised, which places the newborn at risk. Biological birth ordinarily favors the coincidence of factors that provide a suitable fit. Genetic and hormonal priming places a newborn closer to the experiential realm of a birth parent. A baby who "looks just like his father," or whose "chin quivers exactly like his older sister," or who "has the same color eyes as her mother" evokes an uncanny familiarity and ease of bonding that is not present in the case of an adopted child who presents as a completely enigmatic stranger to an adoptive parent.

Such benefits of hormonal and genetic affinity offered by the engrossing experience of pregnancy do not exist for the adoptive parents. Thus, from the start there exists potential risk and vulnerability both for the child and for the parents, which is one possible explanation for why adopted children are encountered more frequently among the clinical populations compared to children raised by their birth parents. For the entire course of their parenthood, the adoptive parents have to contend with the sense that the child they call their own is really not theirs, that it came from another womb and was produced by someone else's seed, and that they have held possession of a precious object that belongs to others. This leaves a gap[1] that may interfere with secure attachment. This gap is not

---

[1]To be sure, such a gap is greater in situations where the child is adopted by parents belonging to a different race. Carlotta G. Miles (Chapter 2) addresses this type of adoption

easily eliminated by assuming all the usual parental responsibilities and constant dedication, meeting every need and making every sacrifice.

> The adoptive father of an outstanding high school graduate who was preparing to leave for college was recounting his son's many accomplishments.[2] He took pride in the son's remarkable achievements and was content with his own role, together with his wife, in raising such an exceptional child. But he could not help lamenting, "So you raise him, love him, give him your name. You want your name to be carried into the next generation. Your father's name and your father's blood. But what good is it when it is not your blood, not your father's blood? Nothing is carried on to the next generation. It all stops here. It's the end of the line." He was grateful for the joy and pride that his son had brought him and his wife. But he was sadly and constantly haunted by the sense that his most precious "possession" was not really his. He felt an unsettling sense of competition with the "real parents" whom he did not know and liked to imagine as inferior and not as worthy as he and his wife. Still he found himself competing with these ghost figures who existed for him everywhere, all the time, as if taunting him and watching him struggle and compete endlessly.

This fantasy of competing with the "real parents" and never quite earning the love one longs for is nearly universal for adoptive parents. They feel the "real parents" have secured this love by virtue of their biological connection to the child. To cope with this sense of failure and shortcoming, they resort to compensatory

---

in great detail. Mike Leigh's movie *Secrets and Lies*, emphasizing the role of nurture over nature in such circumstances, is also important in this context.

[2] The clinical material cited in this chapter comes from Dr. Etezady's practice.

devaluation of the biological parents and, by extension, of their offspring, whom they regard as the recipient of their good will and grace even if undeserving. Many adoptive parents of children who exhibit severe behavioral disturbances see the real culprit as the genetic endowment and the blood line that inevitably made the child prone to evil and doomed to failure, thus liberating them from the pain of guilt and self-blame and providing solace and reassurance as rewards for their loving care and devotion over the years.

IMPACT ON THE ADOPTED CHILD

A child's sense of identity and view of himself begins with the body self. The mental representations of the body and its interactions with its human environment forms an indispensable background against which a progressively well-defined sense of self begins to form. This sense of self grows out of an initial undifferentiated state in which boundaries are indistinct and the self and the primary object are not clearly distinguished (Jacobson 1964, Mahler et al. 1975). Once the sense of self is clearly established, the mental representations of the love objects are also more distinct, and their specific qualities become increasingly more important. For the child a sense of who he is and the quality of his self-regard is inexorably tied to the perceived qualities of the parents (Kohut 1971). The expression "I am my children's mother (or father)" stresses the personal, moral, and social dedication of parents to their children. It bespeaks an essential state of self-definition for the mother and the father. It is in reality the mirror image of a confirmation we have all sensed in the depths of our being, that we are the children of our parents. Children see their own value and validity in the unquestionable certainty that they belong to that one and only particular individual who is their parent. Who the parents are, how they look or behave, and what they do and believe become and remain the bedrock of the child's experience of himself and his core identity and self-view.

Many children seem to suddenly collapse and suffer consequences long after an event that results in sudden disillusionment in a parent. In these circumstances the pain is great, the aftereffects are long-lasting, and the recovery is usually extremely slow and incomplete. The loss of a parent is devastating for the same reason, even though the two conditions are of a different order of magnitude. The ever-present questions, Who am I? and Who do I *really* belong to?, forever haunt the adopted child and assume varying shades of intensity at different developmental levels. When the adoptive parents are able to deal with these important questions and their unsettling reverberations through empathy and understanding of the child's needs, the child better can deal with the effects. Adopted children with preexisting vulnerabilities, living with adoptive parents who are overwhelmed with their complicated circumstances, are at greater risk. A particularly disturbing time is early adolescence, when the reworking of one's sense of identity becomes an essential developmental challenge (Sorosky et al. 1975). Still another developmental crisis occurs at the end of adolescence and the beginning of adulthood, when the identity is expected to consolidate. Around these two periods, many adopted children begin to launch significant efforts toward locating their biological parents. Some individuals who have failed to look for their biological parents in adolescence may do so as they prepare to marry or have their own children.

In younger children, along with the fantasy that "I must be bad or my parents would not have given me away" (Schechter 1967), are other common restitutive fantasies that are comforting and serve as a salve, but never quite erase self-doubt and the questioning of one's own worth. These restitutive fantasies place the individual in an imaginary world of glamour and omnipotent wish fulfillment far removed from fear, loss, helplessness, and abandonment (Sherick 1983, Wieder 1977). One such individual, for example, clung knowingly to a false belief that his real parents were royalty and that he had access to this unbounded love, power, and endless influence if he needed it.

In cases when, as it often happens, adoptive parents suddenly and with delight discover that they are having their own baby after all, the normal trauma of the birth of a sibling is even greater for the adopted child. This additional intensity is due to the fact that the adopted child is not as securely anchored in his relationship with the parents. His own aggression, as well as any situational disruption in this relationship, becomes a greater threat to his security as compared to a natural child. When this added risk combines with previously existing vulnerability of the adopted child, the result can well be a disturbed development. Usually, the biological child, under these circumstances, ends up being better adjusted. It is easy to see how this constellation can easily confirm the notion that the disturbance emanates from the child's poor heritage, his inferior blood, or the bad seed he came from.

IMPACT ON SIBLINGS

A brother or sister can be a valuable asset. Having someone to look up to, someone older to look after you and, when necessary, defend and protect you, is something devoutly to be wished. But rivalry, jealousy, envy, and conflict are inevitable aspects of sibling relations. In families in which there are both adopted and biological children, the children question whether the parents love their own "flesh and blood" more. The biological children then have to contend with victor's guilt on the one hand, and on the other with the fantasy that they too could be given up for adoption (Jacobs 1988). This fantasy, combined with the unconscious guilt over one's "victory," can give rise to anxiety and defenses against this anxiety that may range from regression and passivity to reaction formation and compulsive rigidity. Added intensity and complication will be more likely if the adopted child or biological child has individual vulnerabilities or if the parents' caregiving capacity is impeded by interpersonal, emotional, physical, or social problems.

A couple with chronic conflict and marital discord hoped to improve their failing marriage by adopting a child from an orphanage in another country. Soon they learned that their adopted child was severely disturbed, presumably because of severe neglect and abuse during his infancy at the orphanage. They later became resigned to the unhappy realization that their selfless intentions and declarations of love and devotion would not undo the damage the child had sustained.

Before long, they had their own two children. Their initial delight and exuberance later gave way to the heart-breaking realization that both of these children had severe behavioral and emotional difficulties. The parents subsequently divorced. The older of these two biological children had multiple phobias, was severely regressed, and used many compulsive rituals to contain his overwhelming anger. What brought him to treatment was his acute fear that he was going to die. This symptom had flared up shortly after his adopted sibling needed hospitalization for elective surgery. His fear that he was dying was the result of his guilt, associated with his idea that he and his parents would be better off without the adopted sibling, who did not look like a family member and had been the source of much friction and fighting between the parents.

IMPACT ON SOCIETY AT LARGE

Society at large regards adoption with a degree of subtle ambivalence. The status of an adopted child implies abandonment, illegitimacy, and other sinister circumstances. Adoptive parents stir up fantasies in others regarding lack of fertility (and, by implication, sexuality). At the same time, adoption can also be imbued with qualities of altruism, generosity, and selflessness. People admire or envy adoptive parents for this ability to devote their lives to loving, raising, and providing for children who, through no fault of their own, are parentless. Yet there is a certain amount of skepticism and doubt as to whether these parents really love their adopted children as if the children were their own. Adoptive parents are frequently confronted with this skepticism, and their reactions vary based on their own sense of conviction and on the solidity of their self-regard.

A depressed woman was in therapy. An important determinant in her depression was a profound sense of loss she experienced when her older sister openly and emphatically rebuked and rejected her. The two sisters had always been very close and unusually devoted to each other. The patient was completely puzzled by the inexplicable change in the attitude of her older sister, who was by all accounts good-natured, kind, generous, and highly respected by all who knew her.

The sister had been happily married to an older man who had managed to accumulate considerable wealth before his death. They had adopted a son. (The patient had five attractive and healthy children.) Before adopting, the sister had doted on the patient's children and showed impressive generosity toward them. Sometime later, the sister had made it known that in rewriting her will, she had bequeathed all her wealth to her adopted son. This had created a profound sense of disappointment in the patient who felt betrayed by the sister for favoring a "merely" adopted child over the patient's five children who adored and idolized their aunt. The patient was unable to admit this great sense of rejection and betrayal to herself. She was, therefore, unable to show her pain and sense of being demeaned to her sister. She even thought not making an issue of such great disappointment and not raising the question with her sister would be an indication of her magnanimity and respect for her sister's wishes. Unbeknown to the patient, the sister nevertheless received the message. She clearly understood the patient's unstated protestation that her adopted child was not really hers and, therefore, not worthy of her love and her inheritance to the exclusion of the five nephews and nieces who were flesh and blood relatives. Having received this strong but unstated message, the sister was so exasperated and narcissistically wounded that she could not tolerate the sight of the patient.

Once the patient understood the dynamics of this enigmatic animosity, which seemingly materialized out of nowhere, she was able to understand the source of her sister's hurt, could adjust her expectations, and succeeded in reestablishing a more reasonable relationship with her beloved sister.

CONCLUSION

In this introductory overview, we have surveyed the psychological vicissitudes of adoption. We have discussed the external reality and internal reality, and the dimensions of drives, fantasies, object relations, and ongoing development.

The chapters by Carlotta Miles, Elaine Frank and Denise Rowe, Marshall Schechter, and Martin Silverman, and the respective discussions by Katherine Reed, Jennifer Bonovitz, Ira Brenner, and Paul Viola, along with the concluding commentary by Robert Prall and Henri Parens, discuss additional issues, such as transracial adoption, intrauterine bonding between the growing fetus and its mother, and the role of immigration trauma in international adoptions. It is our hope that this book will deepen and enhance the understanding of the psychological issues involved in adoption, facilitate empathy with all the parties concerned, and help develop beneficial interventions vis-à-vis adoption in both clinical and social settings.

REFERENCES

Bion, W. (1967). *Second Thoughts*. London: Heinemann.

Freud, S. (1908). Family romances. In *Collected Papers*, vol. 5, ed. J. Strachey, pp. 74–78. London: Hogarth, 1950.

Jacobs, T. (1998). On having an adopted sibling: some psychoanalytic observations. *International Review of Psychoanalysis* 15:25–35.

Jacobson, E. (1964). *The Self and the Object World*. New York: International Universities Press.

Kohut, H. (1971). *The Analysis of the Self*. New York: International Universities Press.

Kramer, S. (1995). Parents' hatred of their children: an understudied aspect of cross-generational aggression. In *The Birth of Hatred: Developmental, Clinical, and Technical Aspects of Intense Aggression*, ed. S. Akhtar, S. Kramer, and H. Parens, pp. 1–14. Northvale, NJ: Jason Aronson.

Mahler, M. S., Pine, F., and Bergman, A. (1975). *The Psychological Birth of the Human Infant*. New York: Basic Books.

Schechter, M. (1967). Panel report: Psychoanalytic theory as it relates to adoption. *Journal of the American Psychoanalytic Association* 15:695–708.

Sherick, I. (1983). Adoption and disturbed narcissism: a case illustration of a latency boy. *Journal of the American Psychoanalytic Association* 31:487-513.

Sorosky, A. D., Baran, A., and Pannor, R. (1975). Identity conflicts in adoptees. *American Journal of Orthopsychiatry* 45:18–27.

Wieder, H. (1977). The family romance fantasies of adoption. *Psychoanalytic Quarterly* 46:185–199.

2

BONDING ACROSS DIFFERENCE

Carlotta G. Miles, M.D.

This chapter explores the developmental challenges faced by interracially adopted children and the families who, out of love, seek to integrate such a child into the fabric of their lives. However, any discussion of interracial adoption in America must begin by asking why such adoptions occur, as America is obsessed with and polarized by race, and a decision to integrate a household, whether black/white or white/other, usually carries conscious or unconscious motivations that warrant scrutiny. During the 1960s it was trendy for white families to adopt black babies, just as today it is trendy for white families to adopt Asian girls. For some couples or single parents, there is simply a desperate need for a baby. The average waiting period for a Caucasian baby is seven years, whereas black babies and Asian girls are readily available.

INTERRACIAL ADOPTION
IN THE UNITED STATES

During the civil rights revolution of the 1960s, the races worked hard to resolve their differences. One of the manifestations of good will and good intentions on the part of some white Americans was to make the ultimate liberal move, and show that they were "color blind" by incorporing a black child or children into their nuclear families. The "gift" of white parents and white homes was later attacked by the National Association of Black Social Workers (NABSW), and in 1972 interracial adoptions were halted.

The NABSW passed a resolution characterizing transracial adoption as "cultural genocide." The association claimed that any black child "kidnapped and placed in a foreign environment" with a white family would become a "psychological mongrel" with "chronic schizophrenia" (NABSW 1972, p. 23). This position received a great deal of agreement from many black professionals, and the outspoken position taken by the NABSW led the way to twenty-five years of subtle policies and overt regulations discouraging the placement of black children in white homes. The children of these early adoptions are now adults, and some of the parents were interviewed before I wrote this chapter.

In 1973 the Indian Child Welfare Act granted Native American families and tribes preference in adopting Indian children. The NABSW had lobbied for many years for a similar federal law forbidding transracial adoption. However, with the signing of the Multi-Ethnic Placement Act (MEPA) in 1995 (a federal bill prohibiting all organizations receiving federal funding from delaying or denying the placement of a child on the basis of race), the voice of the NABSW was muted.

According to the National Adoption Information Clearing House, blacks compose 12 percent of the U.S. population, but over 40 percent of the adoptable children, which means that three and a half times as many blacks would need to adopt as other ethnicities. The agency also reports that worldwide there are now 21,200 transracial adoptions. In the United States, no statistics are available, as there is no accurate statistical instrument for measuring this group. Officially recorded black/white interracial adoption has significantly decreased, according to the executive director of the Barker Foundation, a premier private adoption agency in Washington, D.C. Last year, out of a total of twenty-eight placements, fifteen were placed with white families. Many such adoptions take place through private lawyers and are therefore not necessarily included in adoption statistics. The executive director also states that several significant changes have taken place in the adoption world of today. After the heated skirmishes of the 1970s, the Barker Foundation paid increased attention to the recruitment of black families. Perceived roadblocks to the adoption process were removed, and the agency made every effort to become more user friendly to all inquirers of color.

Traditionally, there has been resistance by American blacks to adopting children outside the family. In my work, I have found black men extremely resistant to accepting another man's child. This could be an outgrowth of the black family situation during slavery, when black men were forced to see their wives pregnant with white men's children and were unable to do anything about it. In the past, most black adoptions entailed children from the extended family. However, in the upper classes, there are no such children available, and some couples remain childless due to the reluctance of the husband to adopt children at all and the resistance of both husband and wife to adopting children of strangers.

Black couples are not interested in adopting white children, although occasionally, a black foster mother fights to legally adopt the white child she has cared for in foster care. This situation often makes headlines, since there is always a vigorous debate about the suitability of a black household for the raising of a white child. Interracial children are easily placed in black homes or with interracial couples seeking to adopt.

THE PROSPECTIVE PARENTS

Unlike same-race adoptions, transracial adoptions are overdetermined. Parents can feel that they are making a sociologically significant contribution by helping children from other races find a loving home. In America members of the "other" race are often idealized or demonized or, at the very least, stereotyped. It is this stereotyping that plays a role in the choice of child to adopt. In the 1960s whites were eager to love, help, and sleep with black people, often idealizing our good characteristics and ignoring our short-comings. The civil rights movement raised the consciousness of white America, and the ugliness of the violence associated with integration in parts of the Deep South made northern whites feel guilty of having ignored the black and poor. The fantasy was that adopting a black child would make a lot of things better: (1) whites could share their home with a black child and be recognized as liberal and loving people rather than the demonized dominant group shown on the news every evening, (2) adopting a black child would be striking a blow for a "color-blind" future for America, (3) by setting a good example, white adoptive parents could show their natural children what race relationships could ideally be like.

Today, among white adoptive parents seeking a transracial adoption, stereotyping about the child they want still exists. Ac-cording to another agency executive, when white parents show up after ten years of failed fertility studies, they are sad, frustrated, and ready to adopt quickly. They want a baby fast. The most available babies and children are Asian, South American, black, and Eastern European. Very few adoptive parents are able to hear the cautious, educational speeches of the adoption agencies. The focus is on speed, not the need to change a mind set. Some agencies take advantage of the zeal of these parents and simply show them pictures of children whom they can adopt immediately. These parents are given to stereotyping, and their preferences are gener-ally for, in order, (1) Chinese children—easy to get, compliant, not given to anger; (2) Korean children—academically achieving, devoted to parents, will not desert parents later and; (3) Russian children—white, same as adoptive parents. In contrast, South Americans are viewed negatively—stocky, lackadaisical, peasant type, not driven, academically slow—as are black and racially mixed children—possibly drug using, possessing lower IQs, and potentially having learning disabilities.

Despite the above stereotypes, single white women frequently request a Chinese, black, or Hispanic infant for adoption. Many of these women are over 35 years old and are well-educated professionals. Unmarried either by choice or circumstance, they do not wish to deny themselves the fulfillment of motherhood.

White parents who adopt children of color[1] are like other adopting parents in that they need a child to love, and in America, legalized abortion has made white babies very scarce. Thus, white parents consider adopting children of color, and white judges generally do not give consent for white children to be reared in black homes. In contrast, poverty, drugs, teen pregnancy, and the overworked social service system in the United States have made many more black infants available. Third-world countries also provide access to orphaned children of color, and the current plight of Chinese girls has provided a new pool of adoptees.

Transracial adoptive parents generally believe in the concept of "color-blindness," that is, that race shouldn't matter and that everyone should simply see people as human beings. This characteristic is at once honorable and potentially troublesome to the child of color, for if race is not taken into account in a realistic way, then the things that happen to him or her because of race will not be anticipated by the parents, which leaves the child vulnerable.

Interracial adoptive families basically fall into three categories: (1) white families with one or more natural children and one or more children of color, (2) single, professional white Christian or Jewish mothers over 35 years of age with one adopted child of color, and (3) white couples with one black child. The executive director of the Barker Foundation reported that suitability evaluations were done for those parents wishing to adopt outside their

---

[1]For the purposes of this discussion, children of color include black, Hispanic, East Asian, or South Asian children.

race. The most important issues for evaluation are the parents' willingness to change their family's identity, to confront their own racism, to embrace the child's culture and teach him or her about it, to help the child identify with his or her own race,[2] and to ride out the child's anger at having to make this identification shift. Questions are asked to determine the parents' awareness of the need to expose a child to his or her own culture and their willingness to do so (see Appendix).

PSYCHOLOGICAL AND DEVELOPMENTAL ISSUES IN TRANSRACIAL ADOPTION

The Color-Tagging Process

During the first year of life, as babies learn to distinguish one person from another and to define themselves as separate from the mother, another process is also taking place for infants of color. They are visually and sensorily incorporating the skin color of the parent or caregiver. As they define themselves, they will first assume that their color identity is the same as that of their caregiver. Similarly, many white children who are cared for during the day by black caregivers have a first identity that is black. Children who are cared for by caregivers who speak a language other than that of their parents will forever associate feelings of warmth and safety with that language if the caregiver was positively cathected.

In transracial adoption, where the mother is white and the baby is black, Asian, or Hispanic, this process takes on special

---

[2]In my clinical experience, transracially adopted children typically identify with their parents' race rather than their own. Culture is passed on by families. Black children need black adults in order to learn black culture and to complete the identification process. Young black children in predominantly white classrooms do better if at least one other child in the class is also black. Single black children may be at risk in adoptive families where they are the only child of color.

significance. The child grows out of the stage of primary narcissism with the assumption that he or she looks like those around him or her. How do the adoptive parents help the child make a racial shift to his or her own racial identity? Are the parents willing to do so? What are the mechanisms for making it happen?

The Case of Christian

Christian was officially adopted by the white Protestant parents of two biological children when he was 9 months old, although the mother, Mrs. T., had known him for more than 6 months. She met him and his white foster mother at church and "fell in love with him." An interracial child, Christian was very fair skinned and bald at that time. He would not show his mixed blood until later. The adoption process took six months despite his parents' readiness to have him earlier. Mrs. T. noticed that all of the other children who had been in the care of the foster mother had been adopted, except Christian. The parents kept asking the welfare agency to move more quickly; then they realized that he must be a racially mixed child, and that was why the agency was reluctant to place him with them, and also why no one else had chosen him.

Mrs. T. was raised as a Mennonite and was committed to the idea of adopting a third child rather than having another natural child. The social atmosphere at the time was against having more than two children because of overpopulation. Mrs. T. was a social worker in a church-affiliated social service agency. She and her husband, a diplomat, had been living abroad when both their other children, a boy and a girl, were born. Upon returning to the States, they chose to live in an affluent but diverse neighborhood in order to raise their children in an egalitarian environment. There were adopted children in the neighborhood and an interracial couple with two children. Another interracial family with five children lived next door. The father was a Thai doctor, and the mother a white American. It was into this atmosphere that Christian was adopted.

Mrs. T. noted that Christian walked at the age of 12 months. Also, having had two natural children, she noticed that Christian didn't bond easily to her, and she realized that his nine months' bond to his foster mother had been broken and that had affected him. It was difficult to get him to make eye contact with her for more than a second or two at a time and he didn't like to be held by her. He did seem to bond easily to Mr. T. and to his older brother. Mrs. T. worked hard to forge a close relationship with Christian and remembers that it was difficult and took a very long time. (No one had advised her to have the foster mother weaned away from him, rather than abruptly disappear.) She chose to stop working and stay at home during his early years because she was concerned about his "disconnectedness."

Five other white couples who were friends of Mr. and Mrs. T. had also chosen to adopt black children during the same period. They all worked for the same social service agency that Mrs. T. had worked for, and were able to support and bond with each other over the years, often commiserating with each other about the difficulties inherent in raising adopted children and the issues around transracial adoption.

Mrs. T. states that Christian tanned easily, and in the summertime he was brown while his blond, fair-skinned siblings remained pale. He would again return to his paler color in the winter. The summer he was 3 years old, his grandmother took all three grandchildren on a trip through the Pennsylvania countryside. When they stopped at a roadside restaurant, everyone else seemed to be getting served except them. Finally, the grandmother confronted the manager and asked "Are we not being served because he's black?" The answer was yes.

Despite that early experience, Christian never asked

about his skin color until he was 5, when he noticed the difference in color between himself and his sister during the summer. Although his parents told him at age 2½ to 3 that he was adopted, spoke openly to him about adoption and the reasons for it, and read to him books with positive racial themes, he wasn't particularly interested. Once, however, at about age 5 he called to his mother when she was in another room, "Next time, make sure I come out of your tummy."

His parents made every effort to do everything they felt was necessary to give Christian a positive connection with black culture and identity. They socialized with the other five white families who also had adopted black children. (One family had adopted four black children.) The children bonded with each other and all the families felt less different because they were alike. Christian remained uninterested in talking about race and adoption. His parents told him they would give him any information he needed about his natural parents when he reached adolescence. When he was interested, all he had to do was ask.

Nonetheless, adolescence was tumultuous for Christian. At age 15 he hit areas of conflict full blast. He became angry and verbally combative, particularly with his mother. This was highly unusual since this was a calm family, not given to physical or verbally aggressive behavior. An attempt was made to have him see a psychotherapist; he went twice and then announced that he would not return. His mother had the distinct feeling that he wanted to fight it out with her directly and not have an intermediary for their dialogue. During such fights, Christian would scream "You're not my real mother!" His mother replied, "Yes, I am!" He said he looked for people, women on the street who looked like him, wondering if the woman was his mother. He was usually looking at black women. His mother told him, "Your birth mama is a white person." Clearly, Christian had sealed off an area of rage that became intermittently accessible, resulting in an overflow of feelings. Once these tirades were spent, Christian would return to himself for several months.

At 16, Christian became interested in his biological parents. He was not given the promised information, but he did nothing. His parents did not wish to do it for him. They felt that this area of his life should be fully under his control. Now in a private high school, after being in a mixed, but predominantly black elementary school, Christian was one of a small number of black students. He started speaking "ghetto speak," experimented with alcohol, and dated one black girl seriously. Next he was in love with a white girl, and in college dated girls from both races. At 20 he said he wanted to look for his natural parents, but he never did.

Christian married just as he finished college. His then girlfriend was already pregnant. There was no question of an abortion or of not marrying. They had been dating off and on for three years. She was a mixed-race person, just as he was. Her mother was Cuban and Irish, and her father was Native American and Spanish. Christian was present for the delivery of his son and called home immediately to say to his mother, "Mom, he's so white!" She reminded him that he, too, had been very fair-skinned as a baby. Christian has been a very devoted father. His son now looks identical to him at the same age—curly black hair, light brown skin, and dark brown eyes. Christian's mother reports that Christian considers himself black.

The Identity-Shifting Process

Christian survived what could have been a developmental brush-fire, that is, he had two separations before his rapprochement stage. The first separation was at birth from his biological mother and the second was from his foster mother where he was placed until his adoption at 9 months. While separation from the natural mother at birth is now a part of the adoption process, placement with a foster mother is best eliminated in the best interest of the child's development. Studies show that babies are much more bonded to the natural mother, even in utero, than we ever suspected, and the adopted child begins life without any of the biological sensory bonds with the natural mother in place. Successful adoptions prove that this earliest separation can be survived; however, the second broken bond at 9 months is much more critical to Christian's personality development.

Christian's reluctance to bond again was quickly noted by his adoptive mother, who stated that "he wasn't like my other babies at 9 months; he wouldn't cuddle." She was astute in her observations and her concern. One need-satisfying object cannot simply be substituted for another need-satisfying object without the infant's awareness; Christian's foster mother was his true "auxiliary ego" (Spitz 1965). In this stage of symbiosis, the infant "knows" the mothering symbiotic partner. And, in turn, the mother's "primary maternal preoccupation" (Winnicott 1960) with the infant is the symbiotic organizer of the mind.

It was with his foster mother that Christian traversed important boundaries of infant development from primary to secondary narcissism, through the first two months of life, when learning took place through conditioning, into the third month, when memory traces can be demonstrated. We assume he had begun to be able to wait for and confidently expect satisfaction from his foster mother and to repay her with the milestone smiling response that symbolized his recognition of her repetitive, caregiving habits and his memory of her as the important part-object and then object in his infant life. It was with her that his ego was born. By 5 months he had achieved a symbiotic relationship with her. She responded to his cues—his way of letting her know what he needed, what he was pleased with, and what he was anxious about. She, in turn, selected which cues needed immediate response and which could wait. Her judgment and behavior influenced his behavior and helped to determine his personality (Lichtenstein 1963). What we seem to see here is the birth of the child as an individual. Such symbiotic mirroring composes the basis for identity formation.

The last third of the first year marks the beginning of movement away from the symbiotic circle composed of (foster) mother and baby. There is a shift on the baby's part from interest in the symbiotic circle to interest in his body, movement about the surrounding space, and learning about the environment. It was at this stage of separation/individuation that Christian lost his foster mother, the only mother he had known for the first nine months of life. We must ask what developmental effect the loss of this mother had on Christian.

I believe that Christian was placed at risk by the trauma of separation at a point in his separation-individuation process when he was ready to shift out of the mother–child orbit into the world of material objects and other people (shift of cathexis). According to Mahler and Furer (1968),

> serious disturbances of a permanent as well as of a transitory nature of the sense of identity are due to massive cathectic changes of this intricate regulatory process. Under certain circumstances, at particular crossroads of self-differentiation, cathectic shifts of such magnitude take place that the contributions to and hence our feeling of identity may become dissociated. There may be narcissistic withdrawal, a massive shift of libido from object representations to self representations only. . . . Defusion of instincts always seems to generate surplus unneutralized aggression. [p. 68]

Does this explain Christian's lifelong limited ability to attach to women or his intermittent aggressive outbursts directed at his mother during adolescence? I believe so. His wife, too, noticed his inability to gratify her need for intimacy and his tendency to exist more alone than as part of a pair. However, the extent to which he is able to love is due to the restorative efforts of his adoptive mother, who worked hard to bring him closer to her in the first months that she had him. If not for her, his emotional deficits would have been greater.

Christian experienced what many adoptees of color feel, that they don't fit in because they don't look like the other members of the adoptive family. In adolescence, when Christian searched the faces of black women on the street for someone who "looked like me," he was expressing the wish to reunite with the original mother. Alas, his original mother too, did not look like him as she was white, a fact pointed out to him by his adoptive mother. Did this announcement end his fantasy of reunion with his natural mother? Probably. Unlike many adoptive children in same-race adoptions, he had to relinquish the fantasy as a hopeless endeavor, which he did, thereby encouraging the recathexis of his adoptive mother.

The most important factor in Christian's adult life was the birth of his son, for whom he has absolute love and with whom he is able to display and feel complete intimacy. This is the best of all possible examples of a corrective experience. Christian is fortunate enough to have made a marriage that produced a child who looks like him, so at last he has a true, natural relative. This psychological gift enables him to access feelings that heretofore have been unavailable. He becomes able to share his joy with the child, his wife, and his mother, and to further his own psychological growth.

The Case of Rachel

Six-year-old Rachel was brought to me for treatment because of her intense jealousy of her new natural brother. Rachel had been adopted by Jewish parents when she was a newborn. She had a two-years-older brother who was her parents' natural child. Upon meeting Rachel in the waiting room, I was struck by three things—her self-possession and confidence, her warm and verbal relationship with her mother, and the state of her skin and hair. A constitutionally well-endowed, dark-skinned, healthy, and fit little girl, she was dressed in shorts and sandals. Her skin was dry and ashy, and her short, kinky hair was dry and disorganized.

She came willingly into the playroom, displaying curiosity and immediate interest in the dollhouse and its two miniature families—one black and one white. Both families had a mother, father, two older children, and a baby. Rachel immediately organized her own nuclear family, took the little white baby and placed it in its cradle and put it in a room off the kitchen on the first floor of the house. She placed herself in bed between her two parents. I commented, "The baby is a long way away; will anybody hear it if it needs anything?" Rachel replied, "I'm the baby. I'm the girl!" She later placed the baby on the roof of the house and threw beanbags at it. I thought the message was clear.

Rachel was being raised Jewish and had spent the first four years of her life in Israel, where she was surrounded by Jews of all colors and enjoyed tremendous freedom to run and play. She spoke fluent Hebrew, and when her family returned to America, she was enrolled in a Hebrew day school, where she was first in her class. Rachel assumed that everyone was Jewish. When I told her that I would be away for two weeks and we would miss our sessions, she asked if I was going away "for Pesach." I had never heard that word before, so I asked her to repeat it twice. She finally said, rather impatiently, "Passover!" I said, "No, I'm not Jewish." She was very surprised and looked at me with a curious skepticism.

At the same time that I worked with Rachel, I also worked with her parents, who were eager to do whatever would help Rachel maintain her self-confidence. I educated her mother about her need for different skin care and hair care and told her how to do it. I also told her that she needed to have contact with black people on an intimate level, so that Rachel could learn and observe cultural and family patterns in a black context. This was easy for these parents who lived in an affluent neighborhood that had both black and white families.

I knew a family who lived close to them who would not be resentful about this transracial adoption. The two families developed a close and ongoing friendship and the black couple became Rachel's godparents. The black mother became a resource for all kinds of cultural experiences for Rachel's family as well as the person who could recommend skin care products and hairdressers when needed.

Rachel's therapeutic issues were straightforward. She resented being replaced as the baby, and particularly resented being replaced by a boy baby. Her penis envy was rampant, as was her jealousy about sharing her mother with an infant. Since her older sibling was a boy, she hadn't known that babies, too, could have penises, and she felt short-changed in the classical developmental sense. Not once did the matter of racial difference surface.

As her issues were worked out, her sibling rivalry was reduced to normal levels. She needed reassurance that her mother loved her just as much as before the baby. Several times I cautiously suggested that some of her resentment might be because her mother and the baby were "the same color and you are a different color." She would look at me with true impatience for my ignorance and say, "Didn't you know, sometimes white mommies have brown babies, and sometimes brown mommies have white babies?" Chastened, I decided that part wasn't broken, so it didn't need fixing.

However, she soon became very interested in the birthing process and played out the delivery with the playroom dolls—over and over. I saw that it was the adoption issue that bothered her, and recognized her concern that the other thing that the baby had that she didn't was that he had come out of her mother's body and she hadn't. She was trying to reconcile in her own psyche whether this difference was significant or not. She understood that "another lady had done that part for my mommy," but until the baby was born, she had assumed that that was because her mother could no longer do it. When her mother became pregnant with the baby brother, Rachel realized that that wasn't the case.

I attended Rachel's Bat Mitzvah, where she performed brilliantly. She was still self-possessed and brilliant and comfortable in her Jewish identity. I would later receive a phone call from her mother asking if Rachel could come and see me for a few sessions. This time she came alone. A serious and bright teenager attending a predominantly black public school, she wanted to talk about her difficulties with her black friends and her social life with them. She had trouble explaining her family situation to them, and when she did, they didn't respond well. Accustomed to a closely knit Jewish school community where there were a few other parents with adopted and natural black children, she suddenly found herself in the extreme minority with no adequate language to explain her family. She felt more different than she ever had in her life. Her racial identity was solid, her Jewish identity was solid, and her academic life was successful, but she didn't know how to relate to racist black children at school, many of whom were far less advantaged than she and who teased her, calling her "white people's slave," "Oreo cookie," "white girl," and "brainwashed." She was moderately depressed and puzzled.

Rachel remained in therapy for about six months. She was still a very healthy child with a good ego and her therapy focused on identifying herself within the black culture. She had never been exposed to children like the ones she now coped with. While she looked like them, culturally she was a privileged child. She had little in common with many of them except race. She felt guilty about her dislike of them, having had the fantasy that in a predominantly black school she would have a kind of magical experience. She was disappointed. I encouraged her to read the literature and poetry of black authors, some of which was inspirational. I also tackled her fantasy that somewhere out there, there was a perfect world where everyone got along. I told her that the best anyone could do was to create the world they desired, and that that would be within her power when she finished growing up. We focused on her academic goals and her future.

Rachel graduated from high school with honors and was a Presidential Scholar. I saw her in a television ad highlighting academic achievers of the city. Her smile told me she was happy and getting on with the future she and I had discussed. Her parents did a fine job.

Identification Processes and Racial Identity

Racial curiosity first surfaces around age 3, when children ask persistent questions about the color and feature differences of those around them. "Why is that man chocolate?" "Why does that lady have straight eyes?" "When did I turn brown?" It is at this point that the interracial relationship between parent and child becomes more challenging, because the child has noticed that there is a difference between him or her and the most important people in his or her life. Is this the moment to also introduce the concept of adoption? Should it be done earlier? Or later? How can the child's ego best be protected?

Identification takes place between the ages of 7 and 11½. The special significance in the transracial adoption of a boy is that if the father is white, the young black son will not model the behaviors that allow a black man to survive in the racist American culture. While we are beyond such blatant adaptations as avoiding direct contact, we are not beyond the subtle punishments meted out to black males who are confrontational in the same ways that white males are encouraged to be. In the adoption of a girl, if the mother is white, the young black daughter may find it difficult to success-fully emulate or identify with an object who has different physical features and sociological realities.

The next case illustrates a family in which the children's racial identity was never shifted and in which the family practiced none of the known methods, psychological or psychosocial, that would have allowed the racial shift to take place. As a result, the children had both unstable racial identities and poor ego development and self-esteem.

The Case of Karen

Karen, a young black woman adopted at birth in Finland by a blonde, Scandinavian mother and a dark-skinned black American father, brought herself for treatment after the suicide of her younger, 16-year-old sister and only sibling, who was also adopted. She was profoundly depressed and guilty, feeling that she had failed her sister, even though she understood what she had struggled with all her life. Apparently a failed relationship with a new student, a southern white boy, had been the final rejection that catapulted her sister over the edge. My patient felt that her sister sought out relationships with difficult and potentially racist white males in an effort to prove her worth. If she could get the most unavailable white male to love her, then she could prove what their mother had always said—"Race doesn't matter."

This adage had certainly not proven to be true for this patient, after she had left the haven of her nuclear family. She reported always being asked what/who she was and where did she come from, because of her Scandinavian accent. When she found herself in an American college, the question persisted. She had an accent but was phenotypically a black person. When asked what she was, she replied, "I'm Finnish." This elicited negative responses from both black and white students; blacks thought she was in denial about her racial identity, while whites thought she was insane. In therapy she told me that as a child, she and her sister had fought over a yellow towel that they wrapped about their heads, pretending that they had blond hair like their mother. They loved their mother dearly, but there was a disconnect in the identification process where physical characteristics were concerned. There was no pride in their kinky hair, only envy of their mother's straight blonde hair and a corresponding feeling of emotional distance.

Both girls spent their summers in Scandinavia, where they enjoyed acceptance by their maternal grandparents and where their skin color difference was ignored. While my patient dutifully returned each fall to enter school in America, her younger sister pleaded summer after summer to stay in Europe. Neither parent was emotionally available—the father, a remote and cerebral black American who hid his deeply suppressed anger at white America beneath a highly controlled intellectual exterior, and the mother, a puzzled, optimistic European, who deeply loved both her adopted black daughters and who escaped with them to Europe every chance she had. They lived in a northeastern suburban community with few other black families, and the children attended the local, predominantly white schools. They were both very good students, but they were never given the opportunity to learn about race-related topics. When the children were questioned about their accent or their hair (both had kinky, frizzy hair), they were at loss for answers. Neither took the problems home to either parent, feeling that neither one had the skills to help them.

The summer that the younger sister was 16, she begged her parents to allow her to remain in Europe with her grandparents. She was so miserable in the predominantly white public school in America that she did not want to return. Her father refused her request, and the night before the family was to return to the states, she committed suicide.

Karen's guilt over her sister's death was profound. She wished she could have helped her to survive. Much of our work centered around the grief and loneliness she felt at the loss of her "only true friend." We were able to surface the good self–bad self split in Karen's unconscious, which she was able to trace back to early childhood. She recalled telling other children that her mother was coming to school on certain days and everyone feeling excited. At the end of one day, as she walked out of school holding her mother's hand a friend said, "I thought you said your mother was coming today." When Karen replied that her mother had come and that she was right there holding her hand, her friend said, "She can't be your mother, she's white." Karen felt bad, and she felt worse because her mother didn't say anything and because she felt distanced from this mother, whom she loved so dearly. It was at these times that she felt isolated and different and the difference became incorporated into her psyche as "badness." She saw other people like her on television, mostly on the news programs and they were always doing something bad. The news showed killers and rapists and robbers, but never black men in suits and ties, and her father's anger about America underscored her fear—that to be black in America meant you were bad. She wanted to be good, but she couldn't change her skin color and look like her mother.

Karen began to date black men for the first time while in therapy, but the relationships never lasted. She had little in common with the people she chose to date—mostly men from ghetto backgrounds who had a violent side to their personalities. I pointed out to her that she seemed to want to punish her "bad" side by connecting with men who would abuse her. She countered angrily, "I can't please you, I can't please myself, it's hopeless." I asked, "What's hopeless?" and she replied, "I can't learn it, it's too late. The white men who would love my mother aren't attracted to me, and the black men who are attracted to me aren't good for me."

It was very hard for Karen to distinguish between the different kinds of black people. Her education had been mainly through television, and she didn't know where to look for people who were more like herself. When she tried to engage people by talking about her European experiences and by acting like her mother (tossing her hair and wearing pale lipstick) she appeared ridiculous to those around her, and when she attempted to disappear into the white culture and avoid contact with all black people (hoping to avoid painful experiences of rejection), she was reminded that she was black. No one seemed to like her.

THE ASIAN CHILD'S EXPERIENCE

In a poignant article entitled, "How I Learned I Wasn't Caucasian," Enrico (1996) recalls her first day of kindergarten when she and her adopted brother, both Korean, were ridiculed by older school boys and called "Chinese cherries." "They pulled the corners of their eyes toward their temples to form 'Chink eyes' and laughed and asked us if what we had in our lunch boxes was chop suey?" (p. 2). Enrico recalls looking around at the white children she had known and played with since she had learned to walk, wondering where the Chinese children were. As the white children began to laugh, her brother realized what was going on and said with painful awareness, "We're the Chinese people" (p. 2). Enrico continues in the same vein: "My parents weren't trying to pretend we weren't adopted; they just never discussed our identities as Asians. My parents felt the best way for me and my adopted brother . . . to assimilate into American culture was not to dwell on our foreignness. . . . We were Italians born in Korea, living in California" (p. 2).

Despite her parents' best intentions and love, Enrico's self-esteem took a beating that day. "The mocking voices of the kids on the bus had told me that many people thought Asians were second-rate and not as good as whites" (p. 2). She was beginning to learn what too many children of color learn that "to many, I would simply be 'the Asian girl'—my whole identity reduced to 'someone who isn't white'" (p. 2).

Groves (1997), too, enumerates offensive questions asked by other whites when they encounter her with her Korean daughter:

"The father must be . . . what? . . . Japanese?" "Is she yours?"
"Where did she come from?" "How much did she cost?" "Do you
have any of your own?" But the Korean child is not a pet, not a
puppy to be looked at in a distancing way, and this mother, after
going through a phase where she answered such questions in a
friendly way, decided that she shouldn't have to continually explain
her child's difference from her because answering such questions
tells the child that he needs to be explained or justified (van Gulden
and Bartels-Rabb 1995). Groves says, "Choosing not to answer
helps teach your child how to protect her personal boundaries."
She also noted that around 4 years of age her daughter started
becoming much more aware of the physical differences between
them.

The Case of Tam

Tam is a 16-year-old Korean girl adopted from Korea at
6 months by a white American couple. In an interview
with Tam's mother, I found some of the same experiences
chronicled by Groves. Tam's mother also reported being
publicly asked intrusive, sometimes insulting and insensitive
questions, in stores, at parties, and elsewhere: "Does she speak
Korean?" "Is your husband Chinese?" "How much did you
pay?" "What's wrong with you, couldn't you have your
own?"

Because this mother is quite healthy, her answers to these
questions were always appropriate and designed to turn the
intruder in the same direction: "Those are personal issues, and
I don't know you." When asked why she chose a Korean
child, she replied that they wanted a healthy child and Koreans
gave their children up for cultural reasons. That is, they don't
accept the children of unmarried women, and pregnancies
outside of marriage cause a mother to be shunned forever by
her family and the culture. The child would not have a father's
name and the mother would never be able to marry; hence

these children are often abandoned or the mother and child end up on the streets.

Tam's adoptive parents gave no thought at all to adopting a child who would look different from them. They contacted the Asian Services Information Agency (ASA) and adopted Tam through the Holt Agency, a Korean adoption agency. They were delighted with their child and saw no deficiencies in her.

Tam is an only child, very close to her parents and aware of her Asian heritage. Her mother bought her traditional Korean dresses throughout her childhood, used the word *adoption* early on, did Asian workshops to learn Asian cooking, and always subscribed to Korean magazines and literature. Tam was read Asian stories throughout her early childhood and yet at almost 4 years of age she asked her first important question regarding her relationship with her mother: "What was it like when I was in your tummy?" Her mother's answer to this question was very painful for her and for Tam. Clearly she wished she could have told Tam that she had come from "her tummy."

Tam, now 16, asks no questions about her adoption. She seems comfortable with her adoptive parents. Her mother has told her over and over that she was loved by her birth mother, and that when she wants to go to Korea they will go as a family. Tam says she'd rather go to France. She identifies with the fact that her father was born in Europe and has naturalization papers, just as she does, and has a family of origin that lives in another country. She does not feel like an oddity. When her mother was asked how Tam identifies herself, the response was that she identifies herself as a member of her family, by name. The question of race is sidestepped.

The cultural environment in which Tam is being raised is a very receptive one. Her ethnicity is celebrated at her private school and at home. Her family has relationships with three families from the agency who have Korean children, and

Tam is close friends with a slightly older Vietnamese adopted girl who acts as her psychological guide and "sister." Tam has had no therapy and no emotional upheaval, but she has not yet left home except to attend a small, very diverse, sleepaway camp close by. In her protected environment, she is safe from the ugliness of those who are prejudiced against racial difference. She has not yet started dating.

Will Tam face the turmoil of a racial shift at some time in her adolescence? Is her primary identity presently Asian or American white? It's hard to say. There are many transracially adopted children who exist at the midline of the races and who are content. This racial compromise may be tested in the greater world, but with a strong ego some adoptees remain stable. Tam was adopted from an orphanage, so little is known about her early bonds. At this time, she seems quite capable of strong and deep bonds with her parents. She may be protecting these bonds by defensive denial and repression of internal racial conflict. Only time will tell.

BONDING ACROSS DIFFERENCE

The bond formed in infancy between mother and adopted child of color is challenged at around age 3 to 4 in a way that natural and same-race mother–child bonding is not. As the child moves through the separation-individuation process, intrusive questions and stares and mocking remarks such as those experienced by Enrico can weaken the fabric of the mother–child connection by introducing the element of foreignness and a bad-self reflection before the parent or parents have a chance to even bring up the adoption issues. Despite the parents' best efforts to protect the bond, I'm not sure that it can be done in America. But it is not written that the bonds of any adoption must equal the bond of a natural parent. To paraphrase Winnicott, we must focus on achieving a "good-enough" bond.

Even an adopted child of color in a white family that is conscious of the need to promote solid racial identity is at risk for experiencing what could be seen psychologically as a double rejection. First, the natural mother gives up the child. The key question for every adoptee is, "Why did she give me away?"—and then there is the pressure for the child to identify with people other than the parents. Does the child hear the parent saying, "Don't be like me, be like them" or "I don't want you to be like me, I want you to be like them"? Parents in these circumstances must push the concept that children and parents don't have to look alike, and they must help the children understand that many Americans have trouble with that concept.

Jen (1997) explains this parental dilemma with the concept of "trumping": "We all know, it is not only certain ethnicities that trump others but certain colors: black trumps white, for example, always and forever; a mulatto is not a kind of white person, but a kind of black person . . . and so it is, too, that my son is considered a kind of Asian person whose manifest destiny is to embrace Asian things." Her son, whose father is Irish, has fair skin and mixed features, but people see his straight black hair and "know" who he is.

In the United States, white people's notions about race are seldom challenged by the realities surrounding them. The adopted child of color becomes a lightning rod for their reality testing—can a white mother have a black or Asian child? Did she break an unwritten, but universally understood, taboo of white America and sexually cohabitate with a foreign or black man? White racism is rarely explored and hardly ever discussed openly. While people of color are very familiar with the covert and overt acts of racism, whites almost never notice them or feel them even when they are guilty of committing them. So, the intrusive questions aimed usually at the white mother and her child of color are really a means of measuring her, and the stranger wants to know that she did not break a racial taboo and that she "bought" an Asian child or she did a good thing by "rescuing" a black or South American child.

These issues have a grave, but not always insurmountable, effect on the bonding, separation-individuation, and identification processes of the adopted child of color and on the strength of his ego development. The intrusive questions and stares that start early provoke subliminal emotional awareness of difference in the child and can weaken the maternal bond from the child's side. The questions "Where did I come from?" and "Who do I look like?" pushes mother and child apart in a more profound way than in same-race adoptions because difference is always there and noted by the observer.

Parents must understand and carefully handle the fantasy provoked from the outside. They must assiduously avoid the use of the rescue story in order to preserve the child's good self and to avoid guilt associated with abandoning parents and/or relatives in the country of origin. The rescue story can provoke a sense of shame and worthlessness in the child, especially when media presentations of their country of origin consistently focus on poverty and crime. The "bad-self" image is enhanced, for example, by the thought that, in that country, drug dealers are accepted but the child was rejected.

To protect the budding ego, adoptive parents should turn the child's passivity into activity by focusing on some personal characteristic of the child as an infant that caught their attention and promoted the adoption choice, rather than allowing the fantasy of the child's own early helplessness to prevail and thereby produce a damaged or bad self that could get cathected. Adoptive parents must recognized that for many transracial adoptees the relationship with the adoptive parents will be close but painful as opposed to distant but not so painful.

CONCLUSION

Some issues have not been addressed here for lack of space. They include the following: (1) Premature role reversal: children of color protect their parents from their exposure to racial slurs because they don't think the parents can help them or handle the situation. (2) Choice of mate: this is an extremely important adult life issue for the transracial adoptee and is ridden with potential conflicts. To choose a black mate means psychologically killing off the white parents; choosing a white mate can represent self-rejection. (3) The good-self/bad-self ego split: this is inherent in many interracial situations, especially those families, like Karen's, where there is no exposure to other similar families and healthy black role models. It is also inherent in the adoption of South American children, whose predominant role models in America are demeaned civil service or domestic workers.

The main complicating factor, however, remains that mastery of racism in America is hardly understood by people of color. The struggle to be healthy and to raise healthy children in a country that constantly portrays them as "other" and "less than" is indeed a challenge. Therefore, for the American white, liberal though he or she may be, to take on this task is at once brave and foolish. Nevertheless, whether it is love, need, narcissism, or any other human characteristic that motivates the potential white adoptive parent to try, there must be psychological and developmental guidelines to address the needs of the children involved.

The child's ego development in the transracial adoption is not solely the purview of the parents any more than it is in a biological family. What is fundamentally different has already been discussed here. The success of these adoptions relies on the willingness of the parents to educate themselves about white racism, to confront their own inevitable racism, and to do everything in their power to prepare their child to survive and to understand, with as little bitterness and ego damage as possible, the societal ills that can cause the damage. Parents must also realize that constitution plays an important role in any child's development. Ego strength is influenced by constitution as much as by circumstances.

The concept of white supremacy is one such societal ill. It is a three-legged stool held up by economic strength, skin color, and a conviction that to be white is better than being brown, black, red, or yellow. Our American culture is peppered with the evidence of this concept. Black parents, with the use of "race talk," process all aspects of American culture for their children. Healthy black parents do this objectively, simply pointing out to the child the examples in the print and visual media, as well as in family encounters, that underscore institutionalized racism. The child's ego is strengthened with language and coping skills needed in specific situations, and bolstered by examples from the parents' own experiences. At the same time, they are encouraged and told that they, too, can be successful. There is no encouragement of the victim role.

The incorporation of a child of color into a white home demands that the parents confront their own identity—the same identity that gives them a sense of self and self-confidence—and dismantle it and find other means of supporting their self-worth. The child can be the catalyst for this change. But it is not enough to make the child the political symbol for their own goodness. This will only send the child out into the world naked and ignorant and unable to cope with the overt and subtle acts of racism that are the daily challenge for many people of color. If white parents even attempt to point out the institutionalized racism in the environment, does the child of color not feel that he is being asked to identify with the aggressor? If he successfully identifies with the "other" group—the race from which he actually comes—does this fragment his ego? How can he split his loyalties? Is he "sleeping with the enemy"?

Any white parent who undertakes transracial adoption must see this divided highway, and must see, from the child's perspective, how complicated the path is. Still, the parent must persevere in the building of the psychological survival kit. What are the tools that must be placed in the survival kit and how can it be assembled? I suggest the following:

1. Process the environment racially, including the media, slang, dating, and so on, and then carefully teach the language of self-defense. Learn "race talk," which may need to be learned from a black professional or friend. When something happens to the child that makes him or her feel uncomfortable and has to do with race, parents need to be available and able to confront teachers, other parents, or bullies and stand up for the child. When racist incidents happen and are witnessed by whites in the presence of the child, parents need to respond appropriately and not attempt to ignore the situation. Silence implies compliance.

2. Do not insulate the child with a barrier of defenses, trying to protect him from reality and thereby keeping him from developing the self-discipline any child needs to have.

3. Refer to the child by the race that the world attributes to him or her. If the child looks black, then he or she is black.

4. Teach the child that racism exists but is not an excuse for failure.

5. Teach black boys to avoid drawing attention to themselves with law-breaking behaviors, as they may be singled out for different punishment than their white peers receive.

6. Help the mixed-race child to understand that this is not a unique category. In my thinking, most American blacks have about a 20 percent white racial mixture. For the child to avoid embracing his or her racial identity is to imply a judgment of inferiority regarding the group.

To be successful, children of color in America must have healthy narcissism. That is, they must believe they can wrestle the world and win. To feel like a winner, they must have a strong ego, one that is not vacillating constantly between a societally projected norm of perfection based on skin color or country of origin and a bad self composed of the cathected projections of a dominant society seeking to gain its strength by projecting its perceived weaknesses onto those who simply look different.

There is no final position to take on the issue of transracial adoption. Each case must be judged on its own merit. It would be a mistake to use a standard of perfection rather than understand that it is always better for a child to be reared by understanding people who are willing to translate their love into the necessary actions than to be raised in the care of institutions, no matter how well run.

APPENDIX:
TRANSRACIAL ASSESSMENT GUIDE OF THE BARKER FOUNDATION, WASHINGTON, DC[3]

The study process is an educational process and as such should be initiated in a manner that allows self-evaluation by the applicant. At the same time, it is the responsibility of the agency to reach a conclusion and make a recommendation based on the study regarding the applicant's ability to parent cross-racially/culturally.

This assessment guide is to be used as a tool to help guide staff on how to assess all individuals on their ability to foster or adopt a child whose race is other than the applicant's own. An assessment is to be made to determine their capability and disposition to value, respect, appreciate, and educate the child regarding his own racial, ethnic, and cultural background.

This guide is also to be used to assess situations where a child is already in a cross-racial/cultural placement situation. For example, a foster parent who has requested to adopt his foster child who is of another race, culture, or ethnicity needs to be assessed as well as the child. For adoptive placements, the worker needs to

---

[3]Portions of The Barker Foundation information packet are reprinted here with the permission of The Barker Foundation.

complete the assessment and make a placement. The *Minimum Standards for Child-Placing Agencies* requires that an assessment be completed before a cross-racial/cultural placement in adoption is made.

The assessment guide is to be used as an integral part of the family study process. This process is, by its nature, personal and subjective for both the applicant and the worker. Therefore, it is essential that a worker be aware of his/her own biases and attitudes and have access to consultation and supervision throughout the process.

The assessment guide is to be used by the worker to assist the applicant in identifying the applicant's own needs, experiences, sensitivities, motivation, ideas, values, and priorities as they relate to parenting a child of another race, culture, or ethnicity.

IDENTITY NEEDS OF CHILDREN PLACED CROSS-RACIALLY/CULTURALLY

The assessment guide is to be used to assess an applicant's capacity and ability to meet the following unique identity needs of children who live with a family of different race, culture, or ethnicity. In addition to the existing applicable criteria, these qualities are necessary to enhance the normal development of any child in placement. These needs are:

1. To live in an environment that provides the child an opportunity to participate in positive experiences, which include his culture, religion, and language.

2. For association with same race and/or culture adult peer role models and relationships on an ongoing basis.

3. For environmental experiences that teach survival, problem solving, and coping skills that give the child a sense of racial, cultural, and ethnic pride.

4. For a parent who can relate to the child's life and daily relationship to racial and cultural differences and who can respond to those experiences with acceptance, understanding, and empathy.

5. For a parent who accepts the child's racial and cultural ancestry and can comfortably share this knowledge and information with the child.

6. For the child to have adults around who understand what it feels like for the child to look different from his parent.

7. To have a parent that has knowledge of the child's dietary preferences, and skin and hair care needs.

CAPABILITIES OF PERSONS WHO PARENT CROSS-RACIALLY/CULTURALLY

To meet the identity needs of children who live with a family of a race or culture other than their own, it is desirable that persons who parent these children possess the following capabilities:

1. An understanding of their own sense of personal history and how that helped form their values and attitudes about racial, cultural, and religious similarities and differences.

2. An awareness and understanding of racism and how it impacts the child and family.

3. Commitment to and capability of demonstrating empathy with the child's family of origin regardless of the socioeconomic and lifestyle differences between them and the child's family.

4. Capacity and commitment to provide the child with positive racial and cultural experiences plus information and knowledge about his race and culture.

5. Adequate support of those significant to them in their decision to parent cross-racially/culturally.

6. Tolerance and ability to deal appropriately with the questions, ambiguity, or disapproval that arises when people assume that the child is the applicant's birth child.

7. Willingness to incorporate ongoing participation in cross-racial/cultural activities into their lifestyle and participate in race/culture awareness training.

8. Acknowledgment that interracial/cultural parenting makes their family an interracial/intercultural family, which will have an impact on all family members, and that a decision to adopt interracially will make their family interracial forever.

9. Acknowledgment and preparedness to deal positively and effectively with the fact that as an interracial family they will experience discrimination.

10. The skills, capacity, interest, and commitment to learn parenting skills necessary to parent children, including teaching them to understand and accept their racial and cultural identity plus working to change the feelings of children who deny their racial identity.

11. Capacity to learn the skills to meet the child's dietary preferences and skin and hair care needs.

12. Appreciation of the child's uniqueness, and at the same time, having the ability to help the child have a sense of belonging and full family membership.

The assessment guide is intended to be used to promote discussion and exchange of information between the worker and applicant with the goal of the social worker making recommendations regarding the applicant's ability for interracial/intercultural parenting. It is not intended that the questions be asked verbatim.

CATEGORIES

The guide is organized into the following assessment categories:

1. Experiences and understanding regarding the role of race, culture, and ethnic heritage.

2. Motivation and support systems.

3. Community and opportunities for same race/culture role models and peer relationships.

4. Lifestyle and parenting ability.

Within each of the categories are prompts to help you in directing the discussion. These prompts are not intended to be directed as questions.

At the end of each assessment category are suggested study techniques to assist the worker in obtaining the information. These study techniques also provide opportunities for the applicant to experience and learn more about interracial parenting.

In each category the worker is to assess the applicants' experiences, knowledge, demonstration, and use of knowledge, willingness, and ability to change if needed and their ability and willingness to view the situation from the child's perspective.

The conclusions and recommendations reached are to be included in the home study.

SITUATIONS

The situations are provided to give the worker and family additional topics for discussion and thought. Each of the situations correlates to the four main categories of the assessment tool. Below the situations are some questions or prompts to facilitate discussion of the issue addressed in each of the situations. After the prompts or questions are responses you should expect to receive regarding the situations. If the family's responses do not correspond to the suggested responses, then this should assist you in your assessment of the strengths and needs of the family.

Situation 1

Your family has known the Smiths for years. They are good friends and your children grew up together. As the children were growing up, they always played together, participated in activities together, and were close friends. Your African-American son is now 14, as is the Smith's oldest daughter. Your son asks their daughter to go to a party with him as his date. She tells your son that she can't go out with him because he is not white. Your son comes to you questioning why he could be her friend all these years but can't take her to a party.

   What would you tell your son? (There could be responses regarding prejudices, the parent acknowledging the child's feelings, and helping reinforce his self-esteem.)

   How would you, as a parent, feel? (Responses may include the parent feeling angry or helpless.)

   How would this affect your relationship with the Smiths? (Responses may include statements about the family feeling tension between them and their friends, the family addressing their concern directly with their friends, steps taken to work on the relationship with their friends, or terminating their friendship.)

Situation 2

Twelve-year-old Tina, who is a child of African-American and Anglo heritage, comes home from school visibly upset. When questioned, she begins to cry and relates the following events to you:

Her friend, Joyce, told Tina that her mother said it is wrong to mix the races. Joyce's mother said that not only is your family a sin, but because Tina is mixed race, her birth was a sin.

Tina loves to go to church and religion is becoming important to her. She is very troubled about what Joyce told her, and she wants to know if this is true.

What is your initial reaction? (Responses may include statements of anger, shock, and maybe disbelief.)

What would you tell Tina? (Responses may include statements that would help the child understand that we all have different beliefs and maybe using the analogy of different religions having different practices and beliefs, help the child talk about her feelings, respect the child's feelings, and acknowledge that the problem is not hers but the other child's parent's.)

Situation 3

You are at a shopping center with your Hispanic infant. You notice several people looking at you. Two men seem to walk by you several times and finally one seems to purposely bump into you or your wife. He then looks at his friend, laughs, and makes some derogatory remark about you or your wife's morals. He uses several derogatory terms about your child's ethnic heritage mixed with a lot of profanity. Although he is talking to his companion, it is obvious that the remarks are intended for you to hear.

How would you feel? (Responses may include feelings of anger or frustration at the intolerance of others.)

What would your responses be and why? (Responses may result in the family not responding to the statements.)

How will you deal with such remarks when your child is old enough to understand them? (Responses should demonstrate that the family has the capacity to help the child handle these situations appropriately, and awareness of how to respond, and address issues of prejudice that exist with the child at an early age.) What would your responses be and why?

Situation 4

You are grocery shopping and have your toddler of Hispanic and African-American heritage in the shopping cart seat. A woman approaches you in the aisle, smiles at you, and asks, "Is your child adopted?" You reply that she is. She comments, "What a wonderful person you are! God will certainly reward you in heaven and what a lucky little girl she is."

How would you feel? (Responses might focus on the stranger viewing their child based only on the child's race, and might include anger, perception of the stranger as ignorant, and empathy for the child.)

What would your response be to the woman? (Responses similar to "My rewards as a parent are far more than what my child receives from me" or "Thank you." Explain any other comments.)

Note: Different ethnic origins should be substituted in each of the situations to help in the assessment process.

What might be your concerns for your child in interpreting the woman's comments? (A response in which they turn the situation around and educate the person, help the child feel accepted, and acknowledge their love for the child. This is another opportunity for the worker to assess whether the family understands the demeaning feelings that might be felt by the child in such situations.)

Situation 5

You are at a school conference. It is the first one for your African-American child as a kindergartner. Your impressions of your child, as you have watched him with other children his same age, are that he is at least average in his development and perhaps excels in some areas. The kindergarten teacher informs you that your child is in the "low group" in academic areas. She comments that she doesn't think he will need particular special help in school, such as a tutor or a referral to special education services, but she thinks school may be difficult for him. The mother feels the teacher is stating this because the child is African American.

What is your initial reaction? (Responses could be one where the family acknowledges and understands that the teacher has a perception of the child based on the child's race, the teacher indirectly demonstrating her prejudices/anger/disappointment in labeling the child, and feelings of empathy for the child.)

What would your response be with the teacher? (Responses could include some discussion around how they would handle this situation on behalf of advocating for the child, their ability to disagree and appropriately confront the teacher, probing the teacher for why she thinks this, asking for behavioral indicators that confirm the teacher's statements, and a request to have the counselor or principal involved in the conversation.)

What steps might you take in setting the tone for your child's school years? (Similar responses as to the above question.)

REFERENCES

Enrico, D. (1996). How I learned I wasn't Caucasian. *Families with Children from China* 3:2.

Groves, M. (1997). Sometimes racism hides behind friendly curiosity. *Los Angeles Times,* April 13.

Jen, G. (1997). An ethnic trump. Article included in the Barker Foundation information packet. Barker Foundation, Washington, DC.

Lichtenstein, H. (1963). The dilemma of human identity: notes on self-transformation, self-objectivation, and metamorphosis. *Journal of the American Psychoanalytic Association* 11:173–223.

Mahler, M. S., and Furer, M. (1968). *On Human Symbiosis and the Vicissitudes of Individuation.* New York: International Universities Press.

National Association of Black Social Workers (1972). Position paper on transracial adoption. Washington, DC: NABSW.

Spitz, R. (1965). *The First Year of Life*. New York: International Universities Press.

Van Gulden, H., and Bartels-Rabb, L. M. (1995). *Real Parents, Real Children*. New York: Crossroad.

Winnicott, D. W. (1960). Ego distortion in terms of true and false self. In *The Maturational Processes and the Facilitating Environment*, pp. 140–152. New York: International Universities Press, 1965.

3

SEPARATION-INDIVIDUATION THEORY AND INTERRACIAL ADOPTION

Discussion of Miles's Chapter, "Bonding Across Difference"

Katherine Reed, M.D.

It is a privilege to discuss Dr. Miles's excellent chapter on interracial adoption. This is the area of greatest need when one looks at the sheer numbers of children that need homes, in the United States or overseas. The literature on this topic includes a wide variety of information that ties in with the ideas that Dr. Miles has presented. I hope to show how the ideas of Margaret Mahler can be applied to interracial adoption. How does having a child of a different race (e.g., African American, Asian, Native American, or Latin American) affect early parenting experiences? How does it impact on the child's passage through preoedipal, separation-individuation, oedipal, pubescent, adolescent, and young adult development? What is the prognosis for these children?

I will begin my discussion of Dr. Miles's chapter by giving an overview of her ideas. Then I will comment on her three cases, present a few clinical vignettes, and discuss some ideas that have importance to me both as an analyst and as someone who has had experience with adoption in my own family. My mother was adopted in 1919, and my daughter was adopted from Vietnam in

1968 at the age of 3. She is now 34 years old, married, and, in the terms we are using here, an interracial stepmother. Her adolescent years were a time of upheaval, but it has been one of the great joys of my life to see her emerge into the woman that she is today.

I believe the ideas of Mahler and other analysts are relevant to interracial adoption, including international adoption, and its impact on the adolescent adoptee and the adoptive parents. While I agree with Dr. Miles that the concepts she discusses apply to all transracial adoptees, I will focus on white parents adopting an African-American child or an Asian child. I wish to emphasize that being transracial adoptees is just one important aspect of the lives of these children. There are many other influences on them over the course of their childhood that also have profound effects.

DR. MILES'S CONTRIBUTION

Dr. Miles divides her paper into eight areas: (1) motives of the adoptive parents, (2) historical information about these adoptions, (3) the prospective parents, (4) the myriad psychological and developmental issues in these adoptions, (5) racial curiosity in children, (6) the importance of their identification process and identification shift, (7) the bonding across difference, and (8) guidelines to address the needs of these children.

The concepts in Dr. Miles's chapter apply to children in foster homes as well. Too often children who wait for adoption spend time in foster homes that may be positive environments but are only temporary. Mental health providers know that a "good-enough" permanent bond is better than a temporary or series of temporary settings. I like Dr. Miles's concept of the good-enough bond between the adoptive parent and child. This is a useful application of Winnicott's (1960) concept of the good-enough mother. What remains unclear, though, is how does the bond between mother and child relate to the concept of love? Analysts do not talk much about the role of love, but Mahler (1979) did speak of the catalyzing influence of the love object in the individuation process.

Brodzinsky and colleagues (1998) summarize transracial and intercountry adoption outcomes from social science survey research studies. These adoptions have been taking place over the past several decades and there have been positive outcomes.

> At the level of general adjustment, the bulk of the data indicate that transracially adopted children do not suffer negative developmental outcomes, nor do they have negative self-images. These results, however, do not address the greatest concern: will this type of placement interfere with healthy racial attitudes and racial identity? . . . The overall pattern of results is consistent with the conclusion that parents of transracial adoptees who accept their child's racial identification, and who do not isolate their children from the Black community (by living in integrated neighborhoods and sending their children to integrated schools) do raise children who have a positive view of themselves as African American. . . . The absence of clearly demonstrated negative outcomes following transracial placement, at least in the childhood and adolescence years, has led some social scientists to call for an end to agency policies discouraging such placements. . . . whereas others are hesitant on social and philosophical grounds. [pp. 71–74]

Singer and colleagues' (1985) studies of attachment between interracial adoptive mother–infant pairs also address some of these issues of love and bonding. They found a less secure attachment for these pairs than for the natural[1] mother–infant pairs. They hypothesize that these parents may simply need more time to feel comfortable and secure in their parenting role. The unusualness of rearing a child from a different racial/ethnic background may temporarily undermine their confidence in their ability to handle

---

[1]I prefer "birth" mother (or father) to "natural" mother (or father) because, as an adoptive mother myself, mothering my adopted children felt totally natural to me.

the problems associated with this type of family life. "We cannot be sure that the insecurity is only temporary but the most common longitudinal change in attachment classification is from anxious to secure. . . . The majority of studies on interracial adoption indicate that these children adjust very well psychologically" (p. 1549). Interestingly, Singer and colleagues found that interracial adopted infants who were securely attached to their mothers were actually placed for adoption later than the other group of infants. The question as to how these parents view their children, however, remains. Ladner and Gourdine (1995) explore this issue and that of parental motivation. They surveyed white parents of adopted black children and found that only a small number felt that African-American identity was of significant importance. Some of the parents thought of their child as black, but some preferred "part white," "biracial," or a "human being." The children were usually being raised in an all-white community, as if they were Caucasian. As adults, the children felt they had failed to develop the skills they needed to survive in the larger world. Ladner and Gourdine felt that if the white parents' motive is to rescue the children from their black heritage, the children's mental health should take precedence over the white parents' desire to adopt. They agree with Dr. Miles that if an extensive search for an African-American family is unsuccessful, the white parents must be willing and able to identify with not only their African-American child but African Americans in general. The parents will have forfeited their right to be regarded as a "white" family. Otherwise, they cannot optimally insulate the child from societal forces.

One such parent I spoke to said that he and his wife had been motivated to adopt because there were many children who needed homes; they did not see this as a liberal action. The reality is that adoption agencies present many unrecognized barriers to same-race African-American adoptions, in that they have strict requirements for adoptive families, they are not employing minority managers or staff, they charge high fees, and they are poor recruiters of adoptive families. Also, adoptions and children may linger in foster care and thus be older and therefore harder to place.

As white families continue to adopt children of other races, it is important that they understand the unique heritage of their child and facilitate a feeling of pride in their child. Even young children have a concept of their race. My adopted daughter Kelly was 4 when she pointed out an Asian girl walking along the sidewalk as we drove by in the car, by saying, "Look, Mom, there's a Kelly!" Tizard and Phoenix (1993) point out that "to many white people, pride in one's racial background might seem unimportant, or even undesirable. But in the context of a racist society, feeling proud of being black is not analogous to feeling proud of being white. If the majority stigmatize one's color, then to be proud of it is likely to be a protective factor" (p. 35).

Lesaca (1998), who has critically reviewed the pertinent writings of Solnit and Stark (1961) and Brinich (1980), states

> Adoptive parenthood involves difficult [psychological] challenges. [The parents] must resolve the grief for the wished-for biologic child and come to terms with infertility issues. Anger directed toward the spouse held accountable for the inability or the choice not to conceive can taint family relationships. Insufficient emotional acceptance of the adoption alternative may result in a romanticized image of the biologic child who might have been. Failure to work through the loss of the biologic child can lead to feelings of rejection, alienation, entitlement and misdirected anger toward the adopted child, particularly if he or she fails to meet the adoptive parents' expectations. [p. 58]

In interracial adoptions, these tendencies could be complicated by idealization or demonization of the other race. At the very least, negative stereotyping might emerge at moments of crisis, especially in adolescence. This could take the form of concerns about a boy being too aggressive, or a girl being too sexual, or an Asian girl not being expectedly obedient or compliant.

Adoptive parents' negative fantasies about the biologic parents of their child can predispose them to undue concern about the child's behaviors. These concerns can lead to a prohibitive attitude toward developmentally normal sexual and aggressive childhood activities. The resulting scrutiny by the adoptive parents can convey to the adoptee that they have a negative and antisocial image of him or her. This, in turn, can lead to delinquent behaviors on the part of the growing child. Johnson and Szurek (1952) described how parents may unwittingly seduce the child into acting out the parents' own poorly integrated forbidden impulses, thereby achieving vicarious gratification. The resulting superego defect in the child is thus a duplication of the distortion in the parents' personalities. Such "transmission" of delinquency can occur with greater intensity if parents carry within them conscious or unconscious racial stereotypes.

Parents who have adopted transracially often acknowledge that they were initially unaware of the extent of their own prejudice and of the racism in society prior to the experience of adopting, but learned more afterward. Caldwell-Hopper (1991), the white mother of an African-American child, has poignantly written about this unfolding awareness about herself, her family, and her community. Tizard (1977) has documented the impact of racial stereotypes on an interracially adopted child. She describes what one British foster mother reported she did to deal with school prejudice toward her foster child:

> "He went through a very bad patch of being teased. I had to go to the school in the end, because it was upsetting him—being called Nig-Nog and Sambo all the time. I went to see the headmaster, and he said he couldn't do anything about it. So then I called him a 'White honkey!' He was horrified. 'Well,' I said, 'now you know how the child feels.' And then he went and saw the class about it and it stopped. Normally David doesn't mind people teasing him, but it was a bit too much." [p. 207]

Ladner and Gourdine (1995) found that among white parents who adopted Native-American children, some preferred not to acknowledge their children's racial differences, especially if they were biracial. The authors suggest that perhaps Native-American people should have the right to decide whether their children may be placed in white homes.

Such concern about interracial placements must be weighed against the reality of the great numbers of minority children waiting for homes, with some having multiple foster placements. There are also many children overseas living under even more adverse conditions with no hope of finding homes in their native countries.

The attitudes of grandparents and other family members are also important. Blum (1983) referred to a case in which a Jewish couple was told they had almost no chance of conceiving.

> Her parents were Conservative Jews and were overbearing and intimidating. The young couple heard of an infant they could adopt through an obstetrician. The dark-haired, olive-skinned couple were presented with a blue-eyed baby girl whose hair was so light at birth as to be almost white. The grandparents were openly upset about this child becoming a member of the family. When the young parents did give birth to another daughter, this time dark-haired and olive-skinned, the grandparents were ecstatic. They repetitively forgot birthday gifts for the adopted child, while never failing to remember all occasions involving the second child. Such denigrating behavior is not uncommon and has psychological meaning for the adoptive parents and the adoptive child. [p. 159]

I agree with the idea of suitability evaluations and with Dr. Miles's list of criteria for prospective adoptive parents, specifically their willingness (1) to change the white family's identity, (2) to confront their own racism, (3) to embrace and teach the child about his or her culture, (4) to help the child identify with his or her own race, and (5) to ride out the child's anger at having to make the identity shift. The only criterion I would suggest adding pertains to adoptive parents' willingness to support the search for birth parents if the child is interested. Pipher (1994) describes a case in which this issue became the nidus of difficulty between an adoptive child and her parents. Franchesca was a Native-American girl adopted by a white Midwestern family. During adolescence she became quite rebellious, causing her family to feel frustrated and concerned. She was eventually able to tell her therapist that she wanted to learn more about her ethnic heritage but was afraid to tell her parents out of fear of upsetting them. Once she was able to talk with them, they were very supportive of her explorations, and as she learned more and more it seemed to help her develop her identity and restore her self-esteem.

DR. MILES'S THREE CASES

Dr. Miles focuses on certain important psychological and developmental issues in the presentation of her clinical material. Included in these are the color-tagging process and the identity shift. As I discuss her cases, I will comment upon these concepts and others.

Christian

The loss of his biologic mother and, at the age of 9 months, the loss of his foster mother, combined with the delay in his placement and the fact that he was not able to see the foster mother again, all left him vulnerable during his practicing stage of separation-individuation. These factors undoubtedly contributed to his difficulty attaching to his adoptive mother. He may have felt more trust for the father and brother because he felt abandoned by his foster mother. We hear about the grandmother's experience of prejudice and about his own expression of the wish to have been the biologic child of his adoptive mother. His issues in puberty and adolescence seem related to his adoption but also to his abandonment at 9 months of age. He wishes to find or have a different mother of his own race to help him feel a bond to his racial heritage and to repair his abandonment. His rage seems tied to both these issues.

We see Christian form a relationship with a young woman whose racial background is also mixed. He rushes into parenthood himself, re-creating the circumstances of his own birth; the difference is that he decides to become a good father to his child. In doing so, he identifies with the parenting of his adoptive mother, who worked so hard to forge a bond with him years ago, and he also identifies with his adoptive father by re-creating his connection to him with the new baby. He has also mastered a sense of his racial identity since he sees himself as black.

I assume from the information we have that Christian's birth mother was white. What would it have meant to Christian to have found his birth parents? How much would it have helped him? Were his adoptive parents ambivalent about his search? How much should adoptive parents help with the search? What would the various meanings of that help be to the child? What would have been helpful to Christian if he had been in therapy with a white or African-American therapist? Were his defiant behaviors motivated in part by unconscious wishes to re-create abandonment or test his parents in this area, which is certainly a common part of adolescence in adopted children?

This case also raises the issue of foster care. The contribution of Hughes (1997), who has worked with adopted children with attachment problems, is pertinent in this context. Applying the theories of Mahler and colleagues (1975) and Greenspan (1989) to help therapists and parents understand reactive attachment disorder, Hughes offers helpful suggestions for parenting under such circumstances. Frank and Rowe (1990) and Weider (1978) have addressed the issue of how and when to disclose information about the adoption to the child. This may be less of a puzzle to the parents of a racially different child because the child may start to ask questions about the differences, and the parents who are empathically in tune with the child can make judgments about how much to tell the child at various stages of development.

Adopted children are naturally inquisitive about their own backgrounds and that of their biologic families. Unfortunately, they have a double hindrance in this regard, as they usually find it difficult to learn their personal histories, and are likely to have feelings of ambivalence about what they might discover. All these issues become even more complicated for the interracial adoptee.

The intrapsychic reactions to adoption are most severe in the later part of the latency period (A. Freud 1965), when, according to the normal disillusionment with the parents, all children feel as if they were adopted (Freud 1908) and the feelings about the reality of adoption merge with the occurrence of the "family romance." Lesaca (1998) applied Freud's (1908) ideas about family romance to the adopted child:

> Unresolved questions about their backgrounds can lead to obstacles in healthy identity formation. A strong identification with an idealized image of their biologic parents sometimes fills the emotional void resulting from these lingering uncertainties. Identification with the idealized biologic parents can compel the adopted child to reject and devalue his or her adoptive parents, which complicates the process of identity formation. [p. 58]

This can become complicated for the child with parents of another race. Wieder (1977) wrote about such fantasies in analyses of adopted children. The child wishes to deny the adoption and establish a blood tie to the adoptive parents. One child imagined he had been cast out into the world, had survived independently, and was rescued by his savior mother, whose presence became necessary at all times. The adoptive mother was moral, ethical, protective, powerful, and asexual, whereas fears of the abandoning biological parents developed, in which the child saw them as corrupt, immoral, sadistic, lower class, and uneducated. This eventually led to extreme dependence on the adoptive parents and anger at them for expectable real-life disappointments. Conflicts carried fearful possibilities of retaliatory re-abandonment.

Frankel (1991) comments about such children's rejection of their adoptive parents and interest in reunification with the biological parents. This is more marked in children adopted at or near birth. These children used the fantasy of reunion as a reparative substitute for an intense but ambivalent relation with the adoptive parents. Frankel felt that this was related to disturbances in the relationship with the parents during the first two years. He did not find this in children adopted after the age of 2. This finding is reminiscent of the findings of Singer and colleagues (1985), that interracially adopted infants who were securely attached to their mothers were actually placed for adoption later than the other groups of infants. Both these findings refute the usual assumption that the earlier placement would contribute to a stronger and less conflicted attachment.

The inner concern of a young Korean adoptee is evident in the following poignant anecdote told by his mother to his therapist:

> He came home from school after doing a project on Korea and asked his mom if she knew how many people lived in Seoul (where he was born), and he told her how many. He then asked her how many people lived in all of Korea. He told her how many millions. He then sat pensively and she asked him what was wrong. He said, "I really do understand about my birth mother not being able to take care of me, but was there no one else in my whole country who wanted me?" [Pavao 1998, p. 48]

Rachel

Dr. Miles's second patient, Rachel, presented with strong sibling rivalry. We do not have information about her birth parents, the motivation of her adoptive parents, the circumstances of her adoption, or the history of her development through the stages of separation-individuation. We do, however, know that she had a recent move from a different country and culture, and was surprised when her mother gave birth because she thought that was not possible. Her parents reacted to her sibling rivalry by bringing her to Dr. Miles for treatment, which turned out to be a very good intervention for her. I wonder if the sibling rivalry would have prompted her family to seek professional help if she had not been adopted or had not been African American.

Rachel seems to wish to place herself between her parents in a normal oedipal way, and far from her new sibling. I am curious about her transference to Dr. Miles. Did she imagine her as a fantasied birth mother? She does assume that they are of the same religion. She envies her brother's gender and position as the baby. If he had been a girl, would the envy have been just as intense in the competition with another daughter? Her interest and wishes about the birthing process are very similar to Christian's. What were her fantasies about her experiences with her black godparents?

As an adolescent, when Rachel felt disappointment in her peers, was this in part a displaced expression of her disappointment in her birth parents or adoptive parents? Was her wish to find a special place a reference to her birth parents, or to the land of Israel where she had lived and done so well during her first four years? Dr. Miles acts as a facilitator of her black identity in her childhood and again in adolescence by introducing her to black people and black literature, a very important role, and one that teaches us as therapists and analysts.

Warren (1992) has shown that there is a lower threshold for referral for psychiatric treatment for adopted children:

> Epidemiological data on a national sample of 3,698 adolescents, of whom 145 were adopted, indicate that adoption significantly increases the likelihood of referral for psychiatric treatment even after controlling for the fact that adoptees display more behavior problems and come from more educated families. This is accounted for by the fact that adoptees are significantly more likely to be referred when they display few problems. Thus, contrary to popular myth and clinical lore, the overrepresentation of young adoptees in clinical settings is not attributable solely to the fact that adoptees are

more troubled. Rather, adoptees do display more problems but they are also referred more readily even after controlling for extent of problems. [p. 512]

I would hypothesize that this would be even more likely in the case of minority adoptees. This can be of benefit to the adoptee but could also reflect unconscious racial stereotyping on the part of the parents.

Karen

In her presentation of Karen, Dr. Miles offers a portrait of a family that did not appropriately address the issue of racial identity. I am curious about several things: We do not have information about the two birth mothers, the parents' motivation to adopt, the circumstances of the adoptions, the ages of the children at the time of the adoptions, and the early years and adjustment of the girls. Did early object loss or other trauma in the early years put them at risk? As Dr. Miles says, there seems to have been a disconnection in the identification process with the mother as far as physical characteristics are concerned. I am also curious about the qualities of the transference–countertransference relationship that Karen had with Dr. Miles. Again, what were her fantasies about her adoption, her birth and adoptive parents, and the tragic death of her sister?

In her work with adopted girls, Elaine Frank (personal communication, 1999) has observed that, at around the age of 7 to 9 years, they want to look like their adoptive mothers. They are probably also wondering about the appearance of the birth mother. Later, the girls don't want to look like the adoptive mothers, but want to look different and better. These are both times that the mother and father need to be able to respond to their daughters in a constructive fashion. This depends on the child, teenager, or young adult having learned to communicate to the parents.

It is also important to understand the double rejection for these children, that is, their "be-like-me or be-like-them" dilemma. The analytic process requires that the person understand such a conflict on an emotional level and that the analyst be helpful in elucidating its unconscious meanings. Understanding the concept of racial individuation for a minority person can be helpful for the analyst. The analyst must also utilize other analytic tools to delve into the uniqueness of the patient's subjective experience of his or her race.

A FOURTH CASE IN ANALYSIS

The following analytic case material comes from the practice of a colleague.

> Danny is a 5-year-old biracial boy who was adopted by a single mother. She is of Scandinavian-American background and is fair skinned and blonde. In the course of his four-times-a-week analysis, Danny disclosed that he worried because the kids at school told him that this could not be his mother. She did not look like him. He must have come from somewhere else. Danny asked his white analyst if there was any way he could change his dark skin so that he would look more like his adoptive mother. He tried using an eraser and wondered whether he could get the "dirt" to come off.
>
> For a long time Danny related any of his troubles at school and in the neighborhood to being dark skinned. "It makes me bad," he said. The external reality, that he lived in a predominantly white neighborhood where he did experience racist comments, gave him no opportunity to identify with other children or adults who were dark skinned and "good." The external situation confirmed his inner bad, black self-representation. He worried that his adoptive mother would want to trade him in for a fair-skinned child, and he did everything he could to provoke her to throw him out. He told his analyst that he was going to prove to her that he belonged

in the trash. He noted that the janitors who emptied the trash were black like him, and this proved that he belonged in the trash can. For weeks on end he rushed around the office like a tornado creating chaos of the furniture and the toy shelves. On occasion he would pause to ask, "Are you going to call the manager to have me thrown out of the building?" He imagined that his analyst preferred white kids, who probably didn't give her as much trouble as he did. After many unsuccessful attempts to have himself rejected by his analyst, he sighed and said, "I guess I can't get rid of you after all!"

Around this time he began to use his sessions to build elaborate space ships and fantasized about returning to his home planet. He told his analyst that he was an alien and he had been accidentally launched into space by his real parents, who were probably searching for him. He was going to try to find a way to get in touch with them by telephone. Using the toy telephone in the office, he tried various number combinations to reach them. At one point he began talking in "a foreign language," which was the way people from his planet spoke. Danny elaborated many versions of this fantasy and often said sadly that he was only visiting planet Earth and didn't really belong here.

Danny tells a truly poignant story. He needs to have the opportunity to experience relationships with other people of his race. He is fortunate to be in treatment with an analyst who will listen to his unique individuation issues. His adolescence will undoubtedly be easier, having had the opportunity to work through some of these issues at such an early age.

TRANSRACIAL ADOPTION
AND MAHLER'S IDEAS

The recommendations that Dr. Miles offers for parents are reminiscent of the recommendations that Mehta (1998) makes in regard to raising children of South Asian or other immigrant families. Mehta describes the different ways in which the young person raised in the United States solves the paradox of culture—through compromise, or through an ethnocentric, an overassimilated, or, best of all, a healthy multicultural identity.

Bowles (1988) has added to the multiple applications of Mahler's theories to different stages of life and to different groups of people. She has written extensively about the development of an ethnic self-concept in blacks and biracial children. According to her, the black family and community serve as a protective buffer zone to recharge and supply refueling units, protecting blacks from the harmful micro-aggressions of the larger society. She sees a developmental impasse when this part of the self is denied. To Mahler's stages of individuation (differentiation, practicing, rapprochement) Bowles adds a fourth task for the black youngster: the establishment of an ethnically defined self-representation. She argues that once the self is separate from others, the child moves into the second phase of self-expansion and enrichment, which is the development of the ethnic self shaped between ages 3 and 5. This sense of self gets firmly grounded between ages 6 and 12 and continues to be shaped over the course of the child's life.

> With separation and individuation fragilely negotiated at age three, the child needs continued affirmation of herself that embraces her ethnicity. Where there is dual parent ethnicity, the child ideally embraces both heritages so that intrapsychic autonomy can be achieved. The embracing of both aspects of her ethnicity will allow the child to retain the relationship with both parents intrapsychically, and to give up the idealized images of the parents, to see both parents more as they really are. The child's ability at this time to assimilate parental functions into the identity system contributes to the child's feelings of confidence, positive self regard and self esteem. . . . For the black child and the bi-racial child, the ethnic self-representation is the end point of separation-individuation, but this final stage for the black and bi-racial child is totally neglected in the literature. [Bowles 1993, p. 426]

Descriptions and testimonials from interracially adopted young people confirm many of these ideas. Brooks (1991), for instance, describes 30-year-old John Raible, who feels strongly about his experience as a biracial child in a white home. He spends much of his time traveling around the country speaking. He grew up in the suburbs where there were few black role models. He says that his white parents believed race shouldn't matter, so they didn't deal with it. But Raible was an outsider at school, and the other kids called him names. He became confused about who he was, and developed low self-esteem. He didn't know where he belonged. Only as an adult has Raible been able to sort it all out. Now, as the single adoptive parent of a 10-year-old black son, he works to convince others of the need for same-race placements. "Because of the racist nature of our society, there are things that only black people can give to black kids," Raible says. "I think if we're looking at adoption as what is in the best interest of children, then we really have to think carefully about how we are going to provide for the needs of children of color, and I think that is in same-race families" (p. 20).

We do not know about other aspects of Raible's experience with his adoptive parents. Were there problematic family dynamics that had nothing to do with the adoption or race? His view represents one type of reaction to this kind of adoption. St. John (1995) represents another view. She was born to a part white and part Native-American mother and an African-American father and adopted by a white couple. At the age of 21, she gave voice to her previously unexpressed emotions.

Throughout my childhood, my family freely acknowledged that I wasn't their biological child. . . . Far from practicing cultural genocide, my family proved sympathetic and helpful when, as a freshman in high school, I went through a period of exploring my heritage. When I immersed myself in books and movies that dealt with Native-American and African-American culture and became involved in the local chapter of the NAACP, my parents responded by making a conscious effort not only to point out people of color who made positive role models, but also to help me be open to different cultures. . . . I've just finished my junior year in college; I'm also a person with a pretty good idea of who I am. That knowledge came in handy during my freshman year, when an attack on a dorm resident assistant of color sparked racial tension throughout our campus. I found myself challenged about which "side" I was on. I didn't like these litmus tests and wasn't shy about saying so. When I became the black-affairs editor for the daily campus newspaper, I tried to offer perspectives that made sense to both sides. [p. 152]

Ladner (1978) presents a 36-year-old African-American college professor, Ray Brown. He was adopted in 1952 by a white childless couple, a minister and his wife, at the age of 13. Prior to that he had been one of seven children who were placed in an institution when their birth mother could no longer care for them. "If I could have made the decision, I think I would have preferred being adopted by a black; my parents tried to do as much as they could for me, but as a black child you need people who are able to sympathize with you as a black individual" (p. 170). Ray Brown is married to a black woman and has two daughters. It was only after he was married that he began to evaluate black–white relations seriously.

The ideas of ethnic and racial identity (Bowles 1988, 1993) and/or hybrid identity (Akhtar 1995) help us to understand why some adopted children have a better adjustment than others. We must remember that race is but one factor in their lives, there being other factors that also influence their identity, self-esteem, and adjustment.

INTERNATIONAL INTERRACIAL ADOPTION

The history of adoptions from Korea, Vietnam, Latin America, Philippines, India, China, Russia, and Romania is both heartrending and inspiring. Each adoption has its own unique history, but many of the ideas discussed above also apply with these children. Some of them come from extremely adverse conditions prior to adoption. For instance, a study of foreign-adopted children by Verhulst and colleagues (1992) found that 45 percent of the sample experienced neglect, 13 percent were abused, 54 percent experienced at least one change in caregivers, 6 percent experienced three or more changes in caregiving environments, and 43 percent were in poor physical health upon placement with the adoptive family.

> The older the age of the child at placement, the greater the probability that the child had been subjected to psychosocial adversities. This association sufficiently explained the greater likelihood of later maladjustment with increasing age of the child at placement. Age at placement, as such, did not contribute to the prediction of later maladjustments, independent of the influence of early adversities. Reliable and detailed information on the child's background and functioning should be obtained prior to adoption. [p. 518]

Winkler and colleagues (1988) and Baldwin (1984) state that racial difference in the family has profound and lasting effects. Such families are challenging society's taboos against intermingling of the races and may be unprepared for the bigotry and cultural and institutional racism to which they are often subjected. They are naive to assume that their love for the adopted child will be sufficient. Baldwin gives the example of Sui Wai Anderson, a young Chinese woman adopted transracially at age 2, who changed her name to Sui Wai, in order to reclaim a part of her Asian identity. She wrote a song describing how she learned to like her face but needed to change her name to be true to her background and her Asian appearance.

At the age of 20 Sui began to establish connections with the local Asian community. She moved to San Francisco's Chinatown for several years. She learned to speak Cantonese and gained some insight into the lives of other Chinese-American people. She thus began a reconciliation between her psychosocial self developed in a white American home and her physical self inherited from her Chinese ancestors. Around this time, she wrote a second song explaining that she needed to know about her background before she could know what she wanted in life.

Baldwin raises the question of whether the resolution of identity Sui achieved in her early twenties might dissolve in the face of future crises. After all, adoption issues do seem to resurface at critical moments of passage from one life stage to the next. In this connection, it is interesting to note that Register (1991) makes a distinction between the two questions "Who am I?" and "What am I?" She points out that the concept of identity entwines both self-concept and ethnicity, that is, how one experiences oneself and how one is viewed by others. Will having a family that is not *what* one is leave one confused about *who* one is? The most important early foundation for the child will be a sense of belonging and feeling loved and lovable. Register quotes Nancy, a Korean adoptee college student: "I do think if you're a minority with white parents it makes you a more interesting person. It gives you a lot of depth. You've thought about some serious things and may be more reflective, and that's an attractive quality" (p. 155).

Occasionally, interracial conflict within one's identity can spur creativity (Gill and Jackson 1983). We see this creativity in such well-known adoptees as Native-American folk singer Buffy Ste. Marie, Olympic skater Surya Bonaly, and basketball star Dennis Rodman, who was raised by a white foster mother.

Register (1991) also describes experiences of international adoptees finding their birth parents. A young Korean adoptee, Colleen, stated,

> "My Korean mother is like an aunt. I don't even consider her my mother anymore. I don't have any close bonds with her, like a mother and daughter bond. I kind of feel sorry for her because I know she would like to have a closer bond, but it's just not there. I'm glad she gave me a good start in life, because I know I was really

loved over there. But for the rest of my life here, I was raised to be an American." [p. 195]

ADOLESCENCE AND YOUNG ADULTHOOD

Adolescence is a particularly challenging time for adoptees. Blos (1967) has applied Mahler's theories to this stage and sees it as a "second individuation." In his view, adolescence recapitulates the first individuation, which is completed by the end of the third year of life. The two periods of life resemble each other since they show a heightened vulnerability of personality organization, and an urgency for changes in psychic structure in consonance with a forward maturational surge.

In the earlier separation–individuation stage the child is hatching from the symbiotic membrane to become an individuated toddler. In adolescence, there are multiple tasks including the shedding of family dependencies and the loosening of infantile object ties in order to become a member of society at large. Not until the termination of adolescence do self and object representations acquire stability and firm boundaries resistant to cathectic shifts. The superego loses some of its rigidity, and the ego ideal matures. A greater constancy of self-esteem and mood is established, which is increasingly independent of external sources. This opens the way for finding extrafamilial love relationships. Regressive and progressive movements alternate, giving the observer of the child a lopsided maturational impression. This can be very confusing to the parent and may have special meanings when the child is adopted and of a different race. Without the successful disengagement from infantile internal objects, the finding of new, extrafamilial love objects in the outside world is precluded, hindered, or remains restricted to simple replication and substitution. The ego weakness of adolescence is due not just to the increased strength of the powerful sexual and aggressive drives, but in large measure to the disengagement from parental ego support. This, too, may be particularly challenging for adoptees in general and even more so for interracial adoptees, for all the reasons outlined above and in Dr. Miles's chapter.

In wholesale rejections of family and one's past, we see the frantic avoidance of the painful disengagement process. Adolescence is the only period when ego and drive regression are an obligatory part of normal development. It is during this time that one tries to come to terms with the trauma of infancy. We have seen what many of these traumas might be for the interracial adoptee. This represents a most vulnerable time for them.

It is hoped the child can mourn the loss of the internal idealized significant objects and obtain a further consolidated object constancy, with the parents being seen in more mixed, human terms. Individuation also implies taking increased responsibility for what one does. A child with adoptive parents, sometimes stepparents, birth parents (known or fantasied), and interracial relationships has a more complicated task of working out this secondary object constancy, choosing a mate, and eventually making decisions about becoming a parent.

Another aspect of adolescence is coping with parental expectations. Unfortunately, parents might try to mold their child into what they want them to be and overlook who the child is or wants to be. The child might assume that this failure to be appreciated is a result of the adoption or racial difference. This is one of those additional factors that can have an enormous influence on a child's developing identity.

If we pool the descriptions of development from Mahler (1979), Blos (1967), Akhtar (1995), Miles (this volume, Chapter 2), and Bowles (1988, 1993), we begin to get a sense of the daunting tasks of adolescent individuation for adoptees. The new, healthy enough, hybrid self-concept will incorporate the experiences of their birth parents, adoptive family, connections to new special people outside the family, their future, their ego ideal, reactions to parental expectations, and their ethnoracial sense of themselves.

SEPARATION-INDIVIDUATION
AND PARENTING

The parents of the interracially adopted adolescent also have to come to terms with the complexities attendant upon the situation. Colarusso (1990) has written about applying the concepts of individuation to the developmental stage of parenthood, describing the reactions of the parent to the child's preoedipal, oedipal, and adolescent years. In addition to such ordinary dilemmas, there will be special challenges and, with their mastery, special joys in parenting an interracial child through these stages, especially the stage of adolescence with its psychological vulnerabilities.

Some of these challenges may be painful for the parents. They may feel anger, rejection, confusion, despair, and jealousy as the child is searching for a multifaceted sense of self. One challenge for the parent occurs when adolescents have contact with others who reinforce different aspects of their sense of self, and they reexperience old traumas and old questions about origins, lost birth parents, and ethnicity. Parents must try not to get pulled into a reenactment of their child's earlier abandonment; the adolescent would of course test them and behave in ways that could provoke reabandonment. Under such circumstances, parents will need to understand that adolescence may be more protracted for these youngsters and stand by ready to be supportive.

Parents might see adolescence as a last chance to mold their child into what they want that child to be. If they feel frustrated in their attempts to control, they may become more rigid in their parenting style or go in the opposite direction and give up on the child and fail to provide needed and appropriate guidance and support. It can be very unsettling to see aggressive and sexual behavior in one's child. This could exacerbate fears and racial stereotyping. Parents may need professional help with these issues, for themselves as well as for their child. It is hoped the parents will be able to engage in the rapprochement toward their child and form their own new object constancy with the young adult as he or she really is, even if the child is not just as the parent might have hoped.

The wheel, however, comes full cycle only as these adoptees approach their own phase of parenthood. Register (1991) describes the decisions that Joy, a Korean adoptee, made as a married young adult:

> "We wanted something of our own, our own flesh and blood. I love my mother and dad dearly. I never wished that I lived with my biological parents. I just wanted my own child. I wanted something of my own that I could say was MY child: He acts like me; he does this like me; he looks like me. I have no future. I have no past. I have no beginning." (Joy has a son now and her wish is satisfied.) "Next time, I would like to adopt. I think it's neat what my parents did for me. I would like to help another child, the way my parents brought me into their home, loved me as their own, and gave me a wonderful life. I told my mom, 'I have the best parents I ever could have even dreamed for. I would like to give all that love and everything that you gave me to another child. I would really like to adopt.'" [p. 197]

Here we see the power of Joy's positive experience and the positive identification she has with her adoptive parents, much like the patient Christian described by Dr. Miles.

CONCLUSION

While race plays a role in the outcome of interracial adoption, many other factors inevitably influence the development of these young people. As is evident in the cases of Christian, Rachel, Karen, Danny, Sui Wai, and others, interracial adoptees are born with different temperaments and resiliencies, and endure varying experiences on their way to being adopted. They might have medical or learning problems. They might have additional abandonments that remind them of the initial abandonment. They might have good-enough or not good-enough bonding and parenting. Their parents might or might not appreciate them as they are and might place difficult expectations on them. They might have parents and other family members with neurotic conflicts or problematic characters. Their parents' marriages might not survive; new adults as a result of divorce could come into their lives. All these events, stressful as they are, might have even more special meaning to a child of a different race.

Each child uniquely experiences mastery, joy, love, humor, sexuality, disappointment, anger, and trauma. Each one interprets and takes meaning out of experiences at varying levels of awareness. Each dreams, fantasizes, and carries these themes and patterns forward through different stages of development. Each develops a superego, an ego ideal, and multifaceted feelings about self and others. As therapists or parents, our most important task is to listen and to be open to the unique experience of the child. This axiom is even more true in the case of the interracial adoptees.

ACKNOWLEDGMENT

I would like to thank colleagues who have been helpful to me in preparing this chapter: Dr. Salman Akhtar, Elaine Frank, M.S.W., Dr. Jennifer Bonovitz, and Dr. Selma Kramer. I also appreciate the ideas shared by the adoptive parents: Martha Anderson, Marjorie Merklin, and Roger Lane.

REFERENCES

Akhtar, S. (1995). A third individuation: immigration, identity, and the psychoanalytic process. *Journal of the American Psychoanalytic Association* 43:1051–1084.

Baldwin, M. (1984). *An exploration of the needs and concerns of Caucasian families who have adopted Asian children.* Unpublished master's thesis, San Francisco Theological Seminary, San Anselmo, CA.

Blos, P. (1967). The second individuation process of adolescence. *Psychoanalytic Study of the Child* 22:162–185. New York: International Universities Press.

Blum, H.P. (1983). Adoptive parents: generative conflict and generational continuity. *Psychoanalytic Study of the Child* 38:141–160. New Haven, CT: Yale University Press.

Bowles, D. (1988). Development of an ethnic self-concept among blacks. In *Ethnicity and Race: Critical Concepts*, ed. C. Jacobs and D. Bowles, pp. 103–113. Bethesda, MD: NASW.

—— (1993). Biracial identity. *Journal of Clinical Social Work* 21:417–428.

Brinich, P. (1980). Some potential effects of adoption on self and object representations. *Psychoanalytic Study of the Child* 35:107–133. New Haven, CT: Yale University Press.

Brodzinsky, D., Smith, D., and Brodzinsky, A. (1998). *Children's Adjustment to Adoption.* Thousand Oaks, CA: Sage.

Brooks, D. (1991). Black/white transracial adoption: an update. *Ours Magazine.* July/August: 19–21.

Caldwell-Hopper, K. (1991). Adopting across lines of color. *Ours Magazine.* July/August: 23–25.

Colarusso, C. (1990). The third individuation: the effect of biological parenthood on separation-individuation processes in adulthood. *Psychoanalytic Study of the Child* 45:170–194. New Haven, CT: Yale University Press.

Frank, E., and Rowe, D. (1990). Preventive intervention groups with adoptive parents and their babies. *Zero to Three* 10:19–25.

Frankel, S. (1991). Pathogenic factors in the experiences of early and late adopted children. *Psychoanalytic Study of the Child* 46:91–105. New Haven, CT: Yale University Press.

Freud, A. (1965). *Normality and Pathology in Childhood.* New York: International Universities Press.

Freud, S. (1908). Family romances. In *Collected Papers*, vol. 5, ed. J. Strachey, pp. 74–78. London: Hogarth, 1950.

Gill, O., and Jackson, B. (1983). *Adoption and Race: Black, Asian, and Mixed Race Children in White Families.* London: St. Martin's.

Greenspan, S. (1989). Ego development. *Journal of the American Psychoanalytic Association* 37: 605–638.

Hughes, D. (1997). *Facilitating Developmental Attachment.* Northvale, NJ: Jason Aronson.

Johnson, A. M., and Szurek, S. A. (1952). The genesis of antisocial acting out in children and adults. *Psychoanalytic Quarterly* 21:323–343.

Ladner, J. (1978). *Mixed Families: Adopting Across Racial Boundaries.* New York: Anchor.

Ladner, J. A., and Gourdine, R. (1995). Transracial adoptions. In *Mental Health, Racism, and Sexism*, ed. C. Willie, P. Ricker, B. Kramer, and B. Brown, pp. 171–197. Pittsburgh, PA: University of Pittsburgh Press.

Lesaca, T. (1998). Preadoption risk factors. *Psychiatric Times*, March, pp. 58–62.

Mahler, M. S. (1979). *The Selected Papers of Margaret Mahler*, vol II. New York: Jason Aronson.

Mahler, M. S., Pine, F., and Bergman, A. (1975). *The Psychological Birth of the Human Infant: Symbiosis and Individuation*. New York: Basic Books.

Mehta, P. (1998). The emergence, conflicts, and integration of the bicultural self: psychoanalysis of an adolescent daughter of South-Asian immigrant parents. In *The Colors of Childhood: Separation-Individuation Across Cultural, Racial, and Ethnic Differences*, ed. S. Akhtar and S. Kramer, pp. 131–168. Northvale, NJ: Jason Aronson.

Pavao, J. M. (1998). *The Family of Adoption*. Boston: Beacon.

Pipher, M. (1994). *Reviving Ophelia: Saving the Selves of Adolescent Girls*. New York: Putnam.

Register, C. (1991). *Are Those Kids Yours? American Families with Children Adopted from Other Countries*. New York: Free Press.

Singer, L. M., Brodzinsky, D., Ramsay, D., et al. (1985) Mother–infant attachment in adoptive families. *Child Development* 56:1543–1551.

Solnit, A., and Stark, M. (1961). Mourning and the birth of a defective child. *Psychoanalytic Study of the Child* 16:523–537. New York: International Universities Press.

St. John, K. (1995). A transracial adoptee speaks up. *Parents Magazine*, July, p. 152.

Tizard, B. (1977). *Adoption, A Second Chance*. New York: Macmillan.

Tizard, B., and Phoenix, A. (1993). *Black, White or Mixed Race?* London: Routledge.

Verhulst, F., Althaus, M., and Verslius-Den Bieman, H. (1992). Damaging backgrounds: later adjustment of international adoptees. *Journal of the American Academy of Child and Adolescent Psychiatry* 31:518–524.

Warren, S. B. (1992). Lower threshold for referral for psychiatric treatment for adopted adolescents. *Journal of the American Academy of Child and Adolescent Psychiatry* 31:512–527.

Wieder, H. (1977). The family romance fantasies of adoption. *Psychoanalytic Quarterly* 46:185–199.

——— (1978). On when and whether to disclose about adoption. *Journal of the American Psychoanalytic Association* 26:793–808.

Winkler, R. C., Brown, D., Vonkepel, M., and Blanchard, A. (1988). *Clinical Practice in Adoption*. New York: Pergamon.

Winnicott, D. W. (1960). The theory of the parent–child relationship. *International Journal of Psycho-Analysis* 41:585–597.

4

ATTACHMENT AND SEPARATION-INDIVIDUATION IN FOREIGN-BORN CHILDREN ADOPTED AFTER THE AGE OF FIVE MONTHS

Elaine Frank, M.S.W.
and Denise Rowe, B.A.

In the ever-changing world of adoption, the need to understand the intricacies of building relationships becomes increasingly important. Of the thousands of adoptions that take place in the United States each year, an increasing percentage are of foreign-born children. Although parents may become quite knowledgeable about the complexities of intercountry adoption, they seem to have less information and time available to experience becoming attached to their children. Adoptive parents have undergone the ordeal of home studies and approval from agencies; have had to travel to foreign lands, learning some language and customs; and have spent enormous amounts of energy and money. In this situation there is little time or attention paid to the attachment process that normally occurs when parents meet the newborn to whom they have given birth.

The foreign-born child, living in an orphanage or foster-care situation, acquires an attachment or nonattachment experience that both becomes his history and shapes his personality. By the time the new parent meets the adoptee, the baby has lived through various relationships and their subsequent attachment losses or disruptions. More understanding of child development and parenting than most new parents have is probably necessary to ensure a healthy attachment and parent–child relationship. Rather than thinking of the child as having "special needs," it may be helpful to explore the special parenting behaviors that will facilitate the establishment of a mutual empathic connection.

HISTORY AND DESIGN OF THE PROGRAM

As members of the Infant Psychiatry Program at the Medical College of Pennsylvania, we began offering groups for adoptive families in 1986. The groups were a variation on the original project begun in 1975 to teach parents about the emotional development of their children from birth to 4 years (Frank and Rowe 1981, 1986, 1990). Although adoption agencies increasingly are providing some postadoption services, very little information on normal child development and attachment theory is included.

In the "After Adoption" parent–child groups, the educational content is based on psychodynamic theories of infant and child development and research, most specifically Mahler's studies and observations of separation-individuation, and the method of a "laboratory classroom," including parents, children, group leaders, and students, was originally developed by Henri Parens. Mahler's theories are augmented by those of Spitz, Erikson, Anna Freud, Fraiberg, Winnicott, and Bowlby, as well as on the insights of attachment and parenting researchers and teachers such as Ainsworth, Brazelton, Greenspan, and Provence. Adoptive family groups meet weekly for one-and-a-half-hour sessions. Groups are also offered in the evening for parents only. Before joining, each family meets individually with the leaders, and individual sessions are scheduled for each family at the end of the semester. Parents can attend for up to three years. Fees are on a sliding-scale basis.

In the sessions, two leaders teach parents to observe their own and the other children. The leaders comment on the children's behavior and its relationship to developmental stages. Discussion focuses on behavior, emotional expression, and communication between parents and baby. Parents can follow their child's development through the process of separation-individuation, and learn growth-promoting ways of communicating with their babies and toddlers. They learn what is normal behavior and what can be expected next. By understanding developmental tasks and timing, they are able "to put themselves in their children's shoes" and to see themselves as facilitators and partners in a lifelong relationship (Frank and Rowe 1990).

After years of seeing adoptive parents and their children in parent–infant groups that teach separation-individuation theory, and of seeing families in developmental guidance groups that combine a clinical application of Mahler and colleagues' (1975) theory with Fraiberg and colleagues' (1975) parent–infant therapy techniques, we became acutely aware of the differences in the way these adopted children become attached to their new families and negotiate the separation-individuation process.

Usually infants progress through the stages of symbiosis and separation-individuation in a more or less predictable and chronological order. Children who are adopted after 5 months of age are experiencing several of these stages at the same time. They simultaneously need to make a connection and are being driven to explore the physical environment.

This chapter describes the attachment process that occurs in these children, and the resulting dilemmas for the child and parents in their quest to become securely attached to one other. The ultimate goal, as for all children, is to achieve object constancy that enables the child to become an independent being who is capable of enjoying intimate relationships with loved ones.

ATTACHMENT

We assume that during the presymbiotic stage, the baby is tuning in to inner and outer stimuli while having his needs met by one or two invested caregivers whom the baby gradually comes to anticipate will satisfy his needs. The mother–baby interaction of expressed need and maternal gratification is repeated over and over by both partners (Bowlby 1980). The baby can then move into symbiosis and feel that he and his mother are one organism, enclosed in a common skin.

Imagine a scene in an orphanage in Russia or South America. There is noise and stimulation but not the beloved, now familiar, face seen by the home-reared baby. He may be reaching out but only receiving a small portion of what he would get with a mother. He may "hatch" (Mahler et al. 1975) but into a confusing and nonattuned human environment. Babies whose reaching-out efforts do not result regularly in an empathic response begin to tune out certain stimuli, for example, noise, lights, and even people, and withdraw, giving up their efforts to extract what they need from others. Fraiberg and colleagues (1975) have written about pathological defenses in infancy that lead to maladaptive patterns of relatedness in children who are neglected or abused. Ainsworth and colleages (1978) describe the distinctive behaviors upon reunion demonstrated by children who are not healthily attached.

Mahler and colleagues (1975) detail how by 5 months of age most babies have highly developed discrimination abilities. They inspect faces and react to both the strange and the familiar in specific ways. At this age, although a baby may smile for other than parents' faces, it is usually obvious to everyone that the best smiles are reserved for the primary relationships. Orphanage babies have been found to show a gamut of reactions from not responding at all to acting comfortable with anyone and everyone in an indiscriminate fashion (Provence and Lipton 1962).

The newly adopted child may have already developed negative or distorted attachment patterns. Because he hasn't had the physical closeness with a specific mothering figure, or is still reacting to the loss of familiar people and environments, he may appear uninterested or unwilling to engage. Parents often report that their child cries inconsolably at times, but is unable to accept their attempts to comfort him. They are reluctant to continue to offer closeness, and they distance themselves from the baby. This, in turn, reinforces the child's maladaptive defenses.

The child's seeming reluctance to engage is exacerbated by his physical ability to move away and by the adult's perception that because he is not a tiny infant he does not need to be kept close by. Most parents are so pleased that their child is not physically delayed that they happily encourage his mobility. Because there is as yet no emotional relationship, the child has little motivation to return to these virtual strangers. The parents are often unaware that their child needs assistance, initiated by them, to stay in proximity. The child has to be helped to relive or indeed experience for the first time those behaviors that occur naturally in the normal infant.

An 11-month-old girl who has been adopted from overseas and who has been in her new home for a month cries for her mother continually and wants to cling and hang on to her. Mother is confused and ambivalent because she fears that the baby is too attached to her. Well-meaning friends and relatives tell her that the baby should be more independent and doesn't need to be held so much or she will become spoiled.

This behavior is not a sign of stable attachment or emotional connectedness to the new parent, but rather is only a sign of the beginning of attachment and an expression of fear and anxiety due to the loss of the previous caregivers and environment. These behaviors are part of innate survival mechanisms that compel the child to hold on to the new caregiver. If her mother is helped to be emotionally available, and understands how this may appear to be at odds with the conventional wisdom about the expected behavior of a child of this age who has been with her family from birth, she will allow the physical closeness to occur, thus fostering the new attachment.

SYMBIOSIS

In situations where early care is fragmented due to the involvement of too many caregivers, or where caregiving is clearly inappropriate and neglectful, even a well-endowed infant cannot get the necessary nurturing reactions to his needs. A baby with any constitutional difficulties will be less likely to experience a normal or "good-enough" symbiotic stage. Babies whose needs are more continually frustrated or are gratified piecemeal by too many people do not have the opportunity to make a specific emotional connection.

Children who are adopted after 5 to 6 months have lost that initial opportunity to attach from birth on into a good-enough symbiosis and most now start the process with their new parents. If they have made any specific relationships, they will react to disruption and experience the pain of object loss as well as starting over. There is the possibility that each time a beginning relationship is lost, the impetus to begin again is lessened. Basic trust (Erikson 1959) is therefore in jeopardy!

As still too often occurs, some babies were fed, held, and cared for adequately, but not on their timetable. Such infants do not learn that their behavior or responses result in predictable reactions from caregivers. The infant might then learn to modify his wishes, withdraw from ill-timed parental efforts to comfort, or react with rage to frustration. That infant might too soon shut down or lessen his attempts to have an impact on the human environment. As a result these young children may still keep trying to get their needs met by their human caregivers, but their methods to achieve that end are transformed into acting-out behavior, or in tantrums, whining, provocative arguments, and aggressive attacks. Some children, in contrast, cease to respond, put up walls, withdraw, or ignore the attempts of peers or adults to interact with them. Sometimes their passive acceptance is seen as good behavior, a sign of adjustment; yet it masks their anxiety and inability to connect emotionally (Van Gulden and Bartels-Rabb 1993).

We have found that some of these babies have also suffered from a poor prenatal environment, malnutrition, or a perinatal stay in a medical facility before entering the orphanage or foster home. Some are delayed in both physical and cognitive spheres of development when they arrive in their new homes, but these delays may go unnoticed because we don't expect many milestones until the second half of the first year, and there is a wide range of behavior considered to be within normal limits.

Groza (1999), who has been following 300 Romanian adoptees since 1992, said that one year after placement, although 20 percent were doing quite well, 60 percent still showed subtle cognitive difficulties, and 20 percent had more intractable cognitive, behavioral, and emotional problems. He quotes Ames, a Canadian researcher, as recommending that "every child adopted from an orphanage be designated as needing extra attention" (p. 50).

Children arriving at between 6 and 15 months of age are often underweight and have bald spots from lying in cribs. They are not creeping or walking and language may be delayed. Mary, who came at 9 months, gained four pounds in a month and did not walk until 16 months. Some children have intestinal parasites that need to be treated, and many have difficulty adjusting to a new diet. Others are unable to soothe themselves to sleep in their unfamiliar surroundings. Consider, for instance, the cases of Mary, Roberto, and Susanna. Until they discovered the parasites, which were first diagnosed in the father, Mary was sickly and cranky and her parents had difficulty getting close to her. They just assumed she was a difficult baby. Roberto arrived from Guatemala at 7 months, and at 2 years was evaluated for both speech delay and articulation problems that showed him to be about six months behind his stated age. Susanna, who came at 1 year and did not walk until 16 months, often chose not to use her practicing-stage skills to leave her mother's side. Emotionally, she was involved in creating an intense symbiosis and did not really begin to separate physically until about

18 months of age, spending most of her waking hours on her
mother's lap.

Adding to the parental quandaries caused by these circumstances is the misinformation about medical facts in general and
about as the children's actual birth dates. Some children are older or
younger than their given birth dates, confusing parents and medical
personnel about what to expect in terms of physical milestones.

FROM OVERSEAS TO ATTACHMENT:
LOVE IS NOT ENOUGH

We know that parents adopting from overseas are motivated to love
and nurture their children, hoping to make up for any deprivation
and environmentally caused delays their children have experienced. Much is known now about the early attachment process.
We have found that a great deal can be done to foster the conditions
necessary for a healthy parent–child attachment to take place.

First, there must be sufficient opportunity for physical closeness. Attachment occurs more optimally when parents allow for
physical touch and hold the child when he or she is hurt, anxious,
angry, frightened, or frustrated. In addition to becoming the
provider of comfort, parents will be encouraging both the emotional and physical development that will eventually enable the
child to begin individuation and separating. Some of these babies
will avoid closeness, or actively resist being held. Others may
appear not to need any special attention. In present-day American
society, independence is so highly valued that, misapplying this
even to infancy, many parents may feel conflicted about holding
their infants, whom they see as too old to be a "lap baby." True, it
is a challenge for adoptive parents to know whether to encourage a
closeness-avoiding child to stay on their lap or to view the child's
movement as an attempt at separation-individuation. The parent
then has to read the infant's experience carefully. Parents of
closeness-avoiding young children are wise to not be so tempted to

encourage the physical mobility and emotional independence of their child until they have some reassurance that the child has attached to them satisfactorily.

In our work with these parents, we teach the parents the importance to their relationship of being able to navigate through the symbiotic stage where the child experiences and perceives the mother and himself as a dual unit within one envelope with no boundary between them (Mahler et al. 1975).

While explaining the nature and behaviors that are evidence of the attachment process, we help them to orchestrate parenting behaviors that will facilitate the repeated mother–baby experiences that mimic in quality and quantity those experiences that the ordinary "good-enough" mother has with her infant from birth to 6 months. Gratifying the expressed and sometimes unexpressed needs and comforting the baby when frustration cannot be avoided—repeatedly, patiently, and lovingly—will gradually over time allow the older baby to become attached even as she continues to catch up with her delayed physical milestones.

Case 1

Lily was adopted from China at 13 months, not yet walking, but raring to go and able to express her opinions, needs, and desires without words. She appeared to attach immediately when her new parents removed her from the orphanage. She clung to them during the long trip home and showed anxiety and fear at bedtime. During the first four to six weeks with her parents, because she was not yet walking, they were able to create the closeness necessary for attachment to begin. She slept in a crib in their room and they carried her about in a cloth baby sling. The sling eventually became Lily's transitional object, and the parents were encouraged to use it when they were not able to be with her, or when she was distressed. Lily would ask for it so that she could lie down on it and get comfortable.

She quickly caught up physically and began to walk alone. Mom and Dad were excited that she was walking, but we pointed out that this accomplishment would also interfere with their newly acquired closeness. We suggested ways of staying physically close. For example, the new toddler fell frequently and we told parents to express sympathy and go to her with a pat or kiss for her minor hurts. When she was annoyed with them and ran off, they went to her, whereas the early practicing infant does not require any reassurance other than verbal or than the simple awareness of mother's presence.

Lily's parents shared the parenting, putting in equal time. As time passed, Lily began to show greater demandingness for her mother's time and attention. She moved to her own room after several months and with the parents' patient assistance, bedtime was more peaceful. However, on the morning when mother was going to work, Lily had a difficult time accepting Dad's presence. It was suggested that Mom arrange her schedule so that she could spend a few more minutes with Lily before she left. This was helpful to Lily, and although she fussed when her mother left, she accepted the transition more easily.

After being here for nine months, one day while being cared for by Daddy, while Mom was at work, she fell and hurt her knee. Dad tried to comfort her and Lily cried, "I just want Mommy." Lily had difficulty accepting Dad's comforting—common in the baby who has reached symbiosis and wants only her mother when emotionally distressed. As Lily's parents were able to use these opportunities to mimic the experiences of early infancy, we were able to see the attachment process begin to unfold in this child. She progressed in her physical and cognitive development, beginning to talk, and she is now showing a delightful personality with age-appropriate contrariness and a strong sense of herself.

Lily's parents were eager to do whatever they could to become strongly attached. They understood the need to work at this from the beginning of their relationship with Lily and were more than ready to provide the kinds of experiences described above. Many adoptive parents need very little encouragement to hold and touch their children once they see the reasoning behind these suggestions. If the baby is not yet walking and is small, there is less conflict about encouraging dependency or allowing her to be a baby when she is already a year old! Sometimes it is necessary to explain these infantile needs to other family members or neighbors who kindly if unwisely suggest that parents treat the child according to her chronological age so as not to spoil her.

SEPARATION-INDIVIDUATION PROCESS IN ADOPTED CHILDREN

After the child has had the opportunity to form a close emotional attachment, that is, symbiosis, in the first six months of life, the separation-individuation phase unfolds during the next two to three years. Mahler and colleagues (1975) describe separation-individuation as two intertwined although separate processes that take place in the psyche of the developing infant and toddler. Separation is the establishment of the child's emotional independence from the earlier symbiotic oneness with the mother. Individuation is the process that results in the establishment of an identity and sense of entity. The separation-individuation process has four subphases: differentiation, practicing, rapprochement, and on-the-way-to-object-constancy (Mahler et al. 1975).

Differentiation

In the differentiation subphase, the baby begins to explore the boundaries between his own and his mother's body. He feels her ears, puts his fingers in her mouth, pushes away with his feet, and arches his back. These physical behaviors allow him to learn the

difference between "me" and "not me," the person versus cloth-
ing, jewelry, and so on. The more subtle mental behaviors can be
observed when the child on Mom's lap visually inspects any
extended family members or visiting strangers. The baby studies the
other faces, then checks back to his mother's face. On his mother's
lap, he can happily engage with the others, but if handed over to
one of them, he becomes more sober, drops his eyes, and if of the
sensitive sort, begins to cry.

We usually do not see this behavior in the babies who arrive
after 5 months of age and we have not observed it in the older
children, but we speculate that those babies with a history of being
cared for by one person may have demonstrated these behaviors at
the appropriate time. However, in the just-arrived babies who are
already sitting and crawling, the observed behavior looks different.
They are often passive or even overstimulated by being passed
around to new family members. They do not protest and people
frequently take this as a sign of independence or sociability (Van
Gulden and Bartels-Rabb 1993).

Case 2

Ten-month-old Jenny arrived at 8 months of age and soon
began to sit up and crawl. As she became attached to her
mother she would explore the toys in her immediate vicinity,
venturing only a foot or so away from Mom. When frustrated
or unhappy, she would call out for her mother and raise her
arms to be held. Jenny looked like a baby of 6 months who,
while learning to sit, falls over, having expected mother to be
behind her and support her. (The adopted toddler who begins
walking soon after arrival can find himself far away from his
mother in a room filled with other people. As he tries to find
her, he searches each face until he locates his parent and hurries
to climb on her leg.)

As she started eating solid foods, Jenny began to feed
mother by poking her fingers into her mouth. She preferred to

explore her mother's body than to venture into play with peers in the group. She was more interested in playful interactions with her parent than in parallel play. When unable to resist the appeal of our play kitchen she dragged mother by the hand to the kitchen so that they could play with it together.

Much of her behavior illustrated the kind of stranger wariness usually seen in a child of 4 or 8 months, rather than 14 months. Luckily, her mother was exceedingly patient and gratified by Jenny's dependence and enthusiasm for sticking so close to her.

Practicing

The practicing stage begins with upright locomotion. The child becomes intoxicated with the pleasures of the world. He is thrilled to practice new skills and situations. He can dart away and appear not to care where his parents are. His preferred distance is about ten feet from mom with his back toward her. If the departure is initiated by the child, all is well, but if the parent leaves him, he is often upset and resistant. When the child feels fatigued or frustrated, he will return to the mother, asking to be picked up and hugged or comforted. This is known as "emotional refueling." Almost immediately, he then wants to get back to his exploratory activities and wriggles to get down.

Adopted children who lived with others before coming to the adoptive parents are in a whole different emotional environment, and the sequence is topsy-turvy. First, they have had to separate from whatever relationships and environment they were in with all the associated disruption and loss. To make new connections they will have to build the new attachment under the influence of those broken images. Usually, psychological separation in early childhood emerges from the experience of basic trust, enabling the child to leave a secure base. This separation is fueled by the child's inner drive to move away from that base to explore the physical environment with its enticements and adventures.

Children who are adopted when they are already mobile are faced with the contradictory pulls of wanting to explore their new situation while needing close physical proximity to attach to their new caregivers. Since these children are not yet attached to their new parents, they are not likely to return to the adults for comfort or refueling while involved in practicing activities. If they do want comfort they may go to anyone indiscriminately rather than seeking their parent.

Even though practicing-stage babies are usually euphoric about their explorations, they tire easily and ordinarily seek out the mother. If she isn't available, the baby becomes low-keyed and seems to be introspective or focusing on inner stimuli. After a successful symbiosis, this "low-keyedness" (Mahler et al. 1975) is less intense and more short-lived. Many mothers do not even notice it, and mention how oblivious to their presence the child appears to be.

Because the newly adopted children have not had a symbiosis, or it occurred with caregivers who are now lost, when they arrive here in the practicing stage this low-keyedness may or may not occur. When we do see it, we wonder if it is not a sign of depressive reaction to the missing people and environment of their past. This is an opportune moment in the parent–child relationship for the parent to initiate the closeness that will enhance the attachment. Because the child is not initiating the closeness, parents who can observe these subtleties can take advantage to maximize this kind of interaction with their child.

Children coming at the end of the first year have already begun to learn the language. Although they soon lose their native tongue, the sounds of the new language are confusing to them at first. There is also a language of love that is being introduced by the parent who interacts with the child, using baby talk. This kind of experience may also be a new one for the child. The parents' verbalizing while physically nurturing and comforting will enable the child to begin to make sense of, or translate, what is being said into what it means to feel loved.

In children who don't demonstrate a depressive reaction, parents must try even harder to find moments when they can be physically close. If a child hurts himself, parents can make a special effort to go to him, comfort him, and "kiss the boo-boo." The child will need to learn that the parents' job is to provide aid and comfort and that a child is supposed to be dependent on Mom and Dad. Orphanage children usually have not had these needs met in a timely way. Staff either encourage self-comforting or independence, or simply do not have the time or ability to meet needs like good-enough parents can.

During the practicing subphase, securely attached children dart away from the mother, return for direct refueling, then dart away again. They are aware of their own emotional needs although they usually appear uninterested in knowing the whereabouts of their mothers. This darting away enables the child to begin to feel autonomy from his mother and to experience the joy of being on his own. He is developing a sense of competency that is firmly rooted in his relationship with his mother. Although the child returns for refueling, he only wants brief contact and avoids being re-engulfed by the mother and her welcoming lap.

Children just beginning to attach who do not participate in the process of darting away and returning may have difficulty acquiring a sense of belonging, or the feeling that someone special (the new parent) cares about what they are accomplishing. The twin concepts of belonging and entitlement are important features of adoptive relationships. *Belonging* refers to the child's conviction that the parents "will take care of me, keep me no matter what, they are my Mom and Dad, and I am an integral part of this family." The home-from-birth child will begin to feel this sense of belonging at 4 or 5 months of age. *Entitlement* is the belief that the adoptive parents have the right to be the child's real parents emotionally as well as legally, providing love and nurturing as well as discipline. This feeling takes time to develop and is usually not complete until the finalization of the legal process. A sense of basic trust or emotional connectedness is the catalyst for the child's venturing into the wider world, doing, learning, and growing as a separate individual. If the adoptive parents understand the importance of this game as an essential part of the attachment process, then they can be aware of opportunities to initiate or encourage the darting away and returning to them. This is hard work because it feels the opposite of what the child may want. Parents who can spend the time and effort to help the newly adopted child feel close much of the time and give the appropriate autonomy at other times will be doing something very important for their child.

It may be that the practicing subphase is the most difficult for parents and children who are experiencing two subphases at the same time. Not only are they influenced by the 1990s' parenting philosophy that dictates children should be independent at earlier and earlier ages, but lifestyles today do not lend themselves to families being together much of the time. Conflicting messages and responsibilities that influence parenting practices in a way that hinders the development of a strong emotional attachment are all too prevalent.

Time is of the essence! The more time parents, especially the mother, can spend with newly adopted children in the beginning of their relationship, the better able they will be to become connected. Understanding how the attachment process evolves, and how long it takes, will allow the parents to be more comfortable doing the necessary behaviors that will ensure that they and their child are starting to become attached.

Rapprochement

The child who begins the attachment process with one person in the first 2 months of life ordinarily builds on the physical and psychological activities and experiences to move through the subphases, especially the rapprochement subphase. Holding, cuddling, kissing, and words of endearment from the beginning are remembered by the child. The accompanying affects are imprinted in the brain, creating for the baby a sense of being cared about and cherished. These feelings help to hold him together as he becomes cognitively more aware of his separateness from the beloved parent. At the start of rapprochement, the toddler moves from "the world is my oyster" (Mahler et al. 1975, p. 27) to an increasing sense of his actual helplessness, how small he is in relationship to the adults and the world. The child is driven to continue to do things on his own, to move out and away, while simultaneously propelled back to his mother who comments that she feels he is "velcroed to my knee." It is as if the child is trying to prove that he is not separate, returning to a symbiotic-like state when, for the child, he and his mother were one entity. The child wants to do things by himself, yet he wants his mother's constant presence, attention, and participation on his terms only. Ambivalence is heightened and temper tantrums occur frequently; Lieberman (1993) says 3 to 30 per hour can be normal. Although beginning to communicate verbally, the child wishes that his mother could read his mind and help him to decide what he really wants. The ambivalence makes the child cranky and whiny. He approaches Mom hoping she will make him feel better, but often she doesn't know what will please him either. Sometimes the best a mother can do is to say, "I understand how bad you feel but I don't know what to do to help you feel better." If they can have some of their old nonverbal closeness and remember their shared empathy, they may both feel briefly better. Sometimes they both feel horrible together.

Coming after the practicing subphase when the child was so absorbed in his activities and new skills, rapprochement often looks like a regression. The darting away in the practicing phase was important because the child had the opportunity to experience autonomy but still be scooped up and reunited with the parent. With his increased cognitive awareness of the perils of separation and the dangers lurking in the world, the rapprochement child needs to stay physically closer to his mother while still driven to separate. The more aware he is of his vulnerability, the harder it is for individuation to occur. "This sub-phase more than any other points up the fact that separation and individuation are two distinct though complementary processes" (Burland 1970, p. 9).

Children who join their family after 18 months and have not had a primary attachment relationship are at risk for not forming a strong-enough attachment with their new parent(s). Without the opportunity to have a symbiosis (which may look really out of place in a child almost 2 years old), they will be handicapped in undergoing the separation–individuation stages as well. Experiencing a "remedial symbiosis" while simultaneously engaging in the behaviors of the more typical 2-year-old allows the child to establish roots in the new attachment relationship. This means that parent and child need to engage in the attachment behaviors of early infancy, such as laptime and getting acquainted with security (transitional) objects.

Case 3

Boris, who arrived from an orphanage in Romania at the age of 24 months, was large for his age and not yet speaking English. He was a handsome boy with a pleasant demeanor and he seemed naturally inclined to cuddle. Shortly after arrival, he became interested in his mother's ski parka with a furry hood. He began to carry it with him and although it is now summer, he continues to hold it close and stroke the fur. His mother was ambivalent about encouraging this closeness and they spent much time with him hanging over her lap, legs dangling. This awkward but engaging portrait of mother–son attachment brought much criticism from relatives and observers. This behavior mimicked the mother–child dyad of early infancy that leads to the establishment of the symbiosis.

Boris's mother was encouraged to provide these experiences when she asked if he was too old to be permitted to spend time on her lap "acting like a baby." A few months passed and Boris began to show the more conflicted behaviors of the rapprochement. He became easily frustrated and dissolved into tantrums, wanted to do things by himself, and directed his aggression toward his mother when she inevitably disappointed him. He would hit and kick her, and she began to worry about his male aggression and the unknown details of his family history.

The mother, a new adoptive parent, had no experience to rely on. Because she didn't know about the orderly progression of the phases, it was hard for her to understand Boris's or her own ambivalent feelings, and she didn't know how to respond to his behavior. She learned about the normal sequence of the attachment process with the ebb and flow of aggression that is to be expected. She was encouraged to employ concrete parenting behaviors that would allow Boris to have the necessary closeness to navigate both the symbiosis and the rapprochement phases. She became more comfortable with his quick changes of mood and ambivalent behavior.

The mother allowed Boris to use her parka as his security object. He sometimes slept with it and wanted to take it with him when they went out. This assisted him in his emerging individuation as it does with infants who get accustomed to an object and use it to bridge their early separations from parents. Because Boris was nearing 3, he would attend nursery school shortly and (thanks to an understanding preschool staff) was able to bring the detachable parka hood with him.

Even when children are adopted between the ages of 5 and 18 months, we often see signs of their being in several subphases at the same time. The earlier they arrive, the more opportunity they have to be treated like a younger infant. If they are not yet sitting, standing, or walking alone, parents naturally minister to them more as if they were infants. Those children who catch up developmentally in a few months often move rapidly into the practicing stage and are impelled to move away or begin to separate from their new parents before they are emotionally ready. When parents are aware of this, they can still maximize their availability to initiate connections even with the child who begins to explore on her own.

Case 4

Cara, born in China, joined her adoptive family at the age of 9 months. Although she sat on her own, she didn't yet crawl. She liked to take in her environment from her position on the floor or from her mother's lap. She was quiet but friendly, and interested in the people around her. Before she began to walk at 14 months, she was able to form a good attachment with both of her parents. Mother was very attentive and available, and Cara enjoyed smiles, hugs, and endless baby games that resulted in making them an enthusiastic symbiotic unit.

Once mobile, she enjoyed a brief practicing period where she delighted in exploring new toys. She traveled with her parents to visit extended family in the Midwest, and happily slept in strange places and socialized with new relatives. Her way of refueling with her mother was to back herself into her mother and plop down in her lap without looking behind her at all. She also developed a strong attachment to an old stuffed teddy bear received from a family friend.

At 26 months, Cara was delightful, spoke English, sang and played by herself, engaged with peers, and was interested in the potty and learning to dress herself. Her rapprochement activities involved bringing toys back to show to her mother, eliciting mother's participation in playing with puzzles, and pretending to cook food and serve it to mother, who eagerly joined in the game.

Because of her age, good concentration, and fine motor development, Cara looked very independent as she played with her back to her mother, seemingly oblivious to her presence. But when she needed to reconnect, she backed up toward her mother, but did not need to get in her lap; she merely sat next her. Occasionally she used words to make sure she had her mother's attention but did not even glance in her direction. When the mother was asked how long Cara had been here, she replied, "Eighteen months." Cara was demonstrating the common rapprochement stage behaviors that we ordinarily see in children who have been with their parents from birth.

Some aspects of the rapprochement stage that pose dilemmas for the adoptive parents are whether the child is too independent because he is not attached enough, or how emotionally available parents need to be with such an older toddler. Although any parent living with a 2-year-old will often feel conflicted, adoptive parents may have more uncertainty about how to respond to the child's progress toward separation and their own ambivalence about giving in to the child's need for contact. Parents find it difficult to give up their wish for alone time when their children appear to be old enough to wait for parental attention. On the other hand, adoptive parents (and many other parents) worry about harming their children if they don't spend every minute with them. The concept of quality time has eclipsed the more visceral old-fashioned idea of simply responding to the child's evident need for attention. Emotional availability, when sought by the child, is considered more essential than planning special times at particular events or places.

On the Way to Object Constancy

The last subphase of the separation-individuation process is open ended, a work in progress, a lifelong journey, with the individual continually negotiating within him- or herself a balance between independence and dependency on love objects. Object constancy has as a defining feature the ability of the child to carry the experience of the early parent–child relationship in his mind when he is not in his mother's presence. Three- and four-year-old children who have successfully navigated the previous subphases are now prepared to venture into the world with a feeling of security and the knowledge that they can return to a loving home base. The securely attached child has acquired basic trust in her parents and other adults, confidence in her mother's love for her, and positive self-esteem. She is beginning to integrate the good and bad mother and self-images in a rudimentary way. She still loves her mother even when they are angry with one another. There may be a momentary splitting when the angry child cannot get what she wants from the mother, but the foundation built upon a positive symbiosis protects the relationship. As the child becomes convinced that the anger will not destroy the mother's love or lead to abandonment, she can tolerate separations from mother without falling apart in her absence. The child can now carry with her the internalized image of the primary relationship, which serves as the template for all subsequent emotional ties. It is probably no accident that the child who has had a transitional object from about 9 months of age often is able to retire it, leaving it at home more, at around the age of 4. The child who has an optimal experience with the first three subphases is now "branching out to the . . . entire psychosocial constellation of his family. [He will be] further influenced by accidental, but sometimes fateful, happenings such as sicknesses, surgical intervention, accidents, separations from mother or father, that is to say by experiential factors" (Mahler et al. 1975, p. 119).

Kaplan (1978) describes the adult's balancing act with object constancy. She defines the baby's interactions with mother as a series of dialogues: the first, when the infant with all needs met experiences unconditional bliss, and the second, when he separates from his mother to learn about real love and acquires the feeling that he is himself and no one else. "All later human love and dialogue is a striving to reconcile our longings to restore the lost bliss of *oneness* with our equally intense need for separateness and individual selfhood. These reconciliations are called constancy" (p. 27).

Roadblocks to Constancy

For children who spent several years instead of months in an environment lacking adequate love and nurturing, it will be difficult to provide the necessary conditions, time, and experiences to make up for the deprivations and allow for the establishment of a normal attachment and separation-individuation process. These children did not develop real basic trust, have never felt real love, and may not have an adequate sense of self. In addition they are confused by all they have lost. Many of them are concerned about the peers they have left behind, asking to bring them along. They have been told that they are coming to America, to join a family in this rich land where they will be lucky to get a mother and father who will love them.

In this condition they must begin at ground zero! They have no understanding of the concepts of family, love, and mother, or of what is required to be a partner in a two-way attachment process with a parent figure. The adoptive parents, on the other hand, have already developed patterns of attachment, experienced all the above abstract concepts, and are exceedingly motivated to become involved in a parent–child relationship with their adored adopted child. They feel they have waited and longed for this experience and have more than enough love to outweigh whatever difficulties relating to the child may bring.

Case 5

Jill came at age 5½ from an orphanage in Russia, where she had spent the last four years with the same group of girls. The caregivers were strict and used corporal punishment to maintain order. There were few affectionate moments between adults and children, supplies were scarce, and the adults were perceived as withholding food and comfort. The attachments were limited to the circle of six girls. Although looking forward to being adopted, when the time came to leave the orphanage, Jill asked if she could bring one of the other girls with her. She was pacified by learning that one of the other girls would be adopted shortly and would also come to the United States, although she would live in a distant state.

In her new family, Jill was an only child, although the parents had raised other children who were living on their own. For Jill, her dreams of America were materially realized. She had a lovely room, toys, and all the food she could desire. Her parents, despite their experience, were dismayed and puzzled by her behavior shortly following her arrival. She became enraged when they denied her anything. She stole and hid food under her mattress, threw and broke her own furniture, and physically attacked her mother when frustrated. She seemed to regard the parents as hired help who were expected to gratify her every wish. After all, what was a family?

She also missed her orphanage "sisters" but had difficulty forming friendships with girls in school. She made one friend, but when visiting her, Jill stole her bracelet and then denied it. Jill had no idea that in order to have a friendship, one has to have empathy and mutual respect, or that taking someone's possession is hurtful and wounding to them. She had little empathy, little sense of self-worth, and no trust that others would satisfy her most elemental needs such as food, let alone affection. To Jill, love meant getting what she wanted and having no one to depend on but herself.

What would it take to transform Jill into an average 6-year-old? Was it even possible? Would she be diagnosed as having an attachment disorder? The first answer is that maybe in three years she could become a more or less average 9-year-old. We know that it takes approximately three years for the newborn to reach the beginnings of object constancy, and the time certainly is not shortened when the child starts at an older age. Also, activities of daily life, including school, make it more difficult for the child to have the kind of intense one-on-one time with the mother as in the case with an infant or small child.

In these situations, parents must embark on remedial or therapeutic parenting. Even Jill's parents, who had raised their other children from infancy, needed more knowledge and guidance to initiate a relationship and to persevere against Jill's frightened and frightening defenses. Mother took opportunities to have physical contact, both the affectionate kind as well as holding Jill when she needed restraining or while she tried to explain to her the rules of the family and of America. "We don't take other people's belongings just because we want them and we don't smash our own furniture when we're mad at our parents." The parents were encouraged to use comforting along with their discipline as they would with a 2-year-old (Parens et al. 1987).

It is hard for children who have already split their world into good and bad entities to eventually realize that they can be angry at the person they are beginning to love. To approximate a rapprochement phase with the older child, one has to verbalize what the younger child is experiencing nonverbally when the mother survives his ambivalent and angry onslaughts. Parents can say, "I love you" but the child lacks the capacity to understand what it means or how it feels. When the disciplinary acts are stronger than affectionate physical acts, the child is thrown back to the hurtful experiences of his past life.

Jill's family could provide both the physical contact and even a kind of approximate rapprochement accompanied by verbal commentary that Jill was capable of comprehending. Although she was extremely manipulative at first, her adequate personality and desire to become an American daughter and belong to her family allowed her to tolerate the closeness to her parents for sufficient time so that she did become attached. She and her parents have had support and therapy at several junctures that focused on building the relationships and processing some of her remembered past. It cannot be predicted yet if Jill will reach a form of object constancy equal to her peers who lived with their families from infancy. Many children with similar attachment histories do not achieve the degree of intimacy in their adult relationships that our society calls mature love.

CONCLUSION

The journey from infant to individual takes about three and a half years. After observing children and their parents during this process for the past twenty-five years, we became aware that the time frame of this process cannot be shortened. It is time dependent and in this case quantity is as important as quality. By applying Mahler's theory to our prevention-intervention groups for adoptive families, we were impressed at how the subphases and their behaviors could be observed in the children who arrived after the age of 5 months. Seeing the overlap and variations that occur in these children helped us to understand the complexity of establishing a parent–child relationship. In these groups there are many different adoption situations. Some children were placed directly from the hospital, others had spent time in foster care, or came from overseas orphanages after several months or years. In this laboratory setting, and in cases of developmental guidance where we saw parents and children individually, we were able to follow the progression of the attachment process.

Some adoptive parents approached us with questions about attachment disorders, sometimes even about very young children under 18 months, or they felt their child was having trouble becoming connected to them. Even when questions about attachment were not expressed by the parents, or other symptoms like aggression were prominent, the underlying themes of attachment, separation, and loss are intertwined within the family relationships and must be considered.

Many adopted children are currently being diagnosed with attachment disorder. A significant number may have characteristics of the disorder but it may be a real disservice to label them with it. Parens and colleagues (1987) describe gradations of relationships as primary (parents and sibling) and secondary (other adults and peer). Where the primary relationships are optimal, the secondary relationships will be adequate as well. Children who come with a history of disrupted attachments will demonstrate gradations in both the nature and quality of their past interactions and in their potential to commence and build a new relationship. These children can be helped to reach their potential if every effort is made to assist and encourage new adoptive parents to learn parenting techniques that will forge emotional ties that will bind them together in a loving relationship. Attachment proceeds over time nurtured by close proximity and innumerable positive interactions between parents and child. Separation-individuation continues throughout life, along with the tension between dependence and independence, and is reworked in the context of one's present experiences, influenced by the past and subject to change in the future (Ames 1997).

It has been our experience that in the after adoption parent–child groups, parents can learn new parenting techniques and gain better understanding of the concepts that enhance relationships. This is best accomplished if they are afforded in-depth, didactic information as well as instruction in observing their children's behavior and communications. When parents can respond appropriately to their children's subtle cues related to their emotional needs, the children gain a sense of closeness and belonging. In addition, the parent–child relationship grows as the parents develop a verbal and nonverbal emotional dialogue with their children. Interactions based on empathy, mutual respect, love and affection, and sensitivity to the child's viewpoint, are the pillars of emotional connectedness. Although we have emphasized repeatedly the tremendous amount of time and effort necessary to build sound relationships, there is no greater gift parents can give to their children.

REFERENCES

Ainsworth, M. D., Blehar, M. C., Waters, E., and Wall, S. (1978). *Patterns of Attachment: A Psychological Study of the Strange Situation*. Hillsdale, NJ: Lawrence Erlbaum.

Ames, E. (1997). The development of Romanian children adopted to Canada. Study funded by the National Welfare Grants Program, Human Resources Development, Canada.

Bowlby, J. (1980). *Attachment and Loss*, Vol. 1: *Attachment*. New York: Basic Books.

Burland, A. (1970). *Ego development during the first three years of life: a summary statement of the selected writings of Margaret S. Mahler, M.D.* Unpublished manuscript.

Erikson, E. (1959). *Identity and the Life Cycle*. New York: International Universities Press.

Fraiberg, S. (1987). Pathological defenses in infancy. In *Selected Writings of Selma Fraiberg*, ed. L. Fraiberg, pp. 183–202. Columbus, OH: Ohio State University Press.

Fraiberg, S., Adelson, E., and Shapiro, V. (1975). Ghosts in the nursery: a psychoanalytic approach to the problems of impaired infant–mother relationships. *American Journal of Child Psychiatry* 14:4.

Frank, E. and Rowe, D. (1981). Primary prevention: parent education, mother–infant groups in a general hospital setting. *Journal of Preventive Psychiatry* I:169–178. New York: Mary Ann Liebert.

——— (1986). Clinical interventions in parent–infant groups around issues related to separation-individuation. *Infant Mental Health Journal* 7(3):214–224.

——— (1990). Preventive-intervention groups with adoptive parents and their babies. In *Zero to Three* 10(5):19–25.

Groza, V. (1999). From Romania: lessons in resilience. *US News and World Report*, September 13, p. 50.

Kaplan, L. J. (1978). *Oneness and Separateness: From Infant to Individual*. New York: Simon & Schuster.

Lieberman, A. (1993). *The Emotional Life of the Toddler*. New York: Free Press.

Mahler, M. S., Pine, F., and Bergman, A.(1975). *The Psychological Birth of the Human Infant: Symbiosis and Individuation*. New York: Basic Books.

Parens, H., Scattergood, E., Singletary, W., and Duff, A. (1987). *Aggression in Our Children: Coping with it Constructively*. Northvale, NJ: Jason Aronson.

Provence, S., and Lipton, R. (1962). *Infants and Institutions*. New York: International Universities Press.

Van Gulden, H., and Bartels-Rabb, L. (1993). *Real Parents, Real Children: Parenting the Adopted Child*. New York: Crossroads.

Winnicott, D. W. (1964). *The Child, The Family and the Outside World*. Baltimore, MD: Penguin.

5

FROM FOREIGN BORN TO FEELING AT HOME

Discussion of Frank and Rowe's Chapter, "Attachment and Separation-Individuation in Foreign-Born Children Adopted after the Age of Five Months"

Jennifer M. Bonovitz, Ph.D.

Drawing on a wealth of observational data from their parent–infant groups, Elaine Frank and Denise Rowe describe the vicissitudes of building an intimate relationship between the foreign-born baby and his North American adoptive parents. Using Mahler's separation-individuation theory as their conceptual framework, they trace the steps required to repair insecure attachments and to remove roadblocks to the development of object constancy. Their poignant clinical vignettes illustrate the differences they have noted in the way foreign-born babies attach to their new parents, and the difficulties experienced by the baby who has had disruptions in early caregiving relationships. They describe the special parenting approaches required by babies who did not have a "good-enough" symbiotic phase with a mothering figure during the first 5 months of life.

In this discussion I first elucidate some of the current psycho-analytic theory and research that support the observations made by Frank and Rowe. There is a growing body of knowledge indicating that the quality of caregiving experienced by babies in the first

5 months of life has a significant impact on their later attachment
behaviors, as well as on their negotiation of each of the subphases
of separation-individuation (Beebe 1986, Brazelton et al. 1974,
Hofer 1987, Stern 1983, Tronick 1980). I next explore some issues
in the practicing and rapprochement subphases, using two examples of work with foreign-born adopted babies to illustrate the
impact of disruptions that occur in the refueling process for babies
who are insecurely attached. Finally, I discuss some of the developmental challenges specific to foreign-born children whose skin
color, facial features, stature, and cultural heritage are quite different
from their adoptive parents. When these obvious differences are
not openly acknowledged, verbalized, and valued by parents, the
adopted child may be unable to form a well-integrated, cohesive
sense of self. Instead, identity formation may be distorted by
fantasies such as that of the "ugly duckling," or the abducted alien,
and the child will remain unable to develop a secure sense of
belonging in the adoptive family and new country (Bonovitz
1998).

THE PRECURSORS OF
SEPARATION-INDIVIDUATION

As Frank and Rowe point out, the foreign-born baby living in
either an orphanage or a foster care situation is from the beginning
of life in the process of becoming a psychological being through a
myriad of interactions with early caregivers. Contemporary research on mother–infant interaction in the first few months of life
suggests that early internal models of self, other, and self-with-other
evolve out of the patterns of interaction with the caregiver. This
interactive process begins at birth and perhaps even in utero. For
example, Stern's (1995) studies of mother–infant dyads suggest that
the mother's fantasies about her unborn baby are powerful in
shaping her relationship even before they meet face to face after
birth.

In 1940, Donald Winnicott startled the British Psycho-Analytic Society when he announced, "There is no such thing as a baby." By this he meant that the infant, and the care he receives from his mother, together form a unit. He coined the term *primary maternal preoccupation* to describe the setting necessary for the infant's constitutional capacities to unfold and "for the infant to experience spontaneous movement and to become the owner of the sensations that are appropriate to this early phase of life. . . . Only if a mother is sensitized in the way I am describing can she feel herself into her infant's place, and so meet the infant's needs" (quoted in Abram 1997, p. 234). Babies who are raised in an institutional setting, or by a foster mother who knows that she is a temporary caregiver, are unlikely to experience this type of emotional investment.

Winnicott's (1965) view that psychological birth occurs as part of an imaginative elaboration of the physical ministering of a mother to her baby is compatible with Mahler and colleagues' (1975) description of the mother as the "symbiotic organizer—the midwife of individuation, of psychological birth" (p. 47). A crucial aspect of early physical care is that it is given within the matrix of a sensitively attuned relationship. René Spitz's studies of children in orphanages dramatically demonstrate that, in the absence of a meaningful relationship with the caregiver, babies who are adequately fed and kept clean and warm nevertheless languish. Grotstein (1991) reports, from an unpublished lecture given by Spitz at Pennsylvania Hospital in 1954, that in fact many of these institutionalized children died by age 4.

Parents adopting from foreign lands frequently do not know the quality of physical or emotional care the baby received either in utero or in the first few months of life. If they are first-time parents they may know little about the intricacies of emotional development. One of the great advantages of their participation in the type of parent–child group described by Frank and Rowe is that they are alerted to subtle signs, particularly in the nonverbal child, that special parenting behaviors are required. More than average, "good-enough" parenting is needed to establish the empathic bond that is essential to activate the infant's innate capacities to develop internal representations of a good self and good internal objects. Schore (1994) argues convincingly that "over the first 18 months of life the infant's transactions with the early socioemotional environment indelibly influence the evolution of brain structures responsible for the individual's socioemotional functioning for the rest of the life span. Such events occur in the one-to-one relationship between the infant and the primary caregiver" (p. 540).

We now know that the affective dialogue between infant and mother plays an important role in the development of early representational capacities. This dialogue is composed of various patterns of vocal, visual, and kinesic exchanges. A number of studies place the origins of self and object structure formation in the first year of life, prior to the emergence of symbolic capacity. Beebe and Lachmann (1988) suggest that infants develop expectancies about how social interactions will go, based on their early representational abilities. When expectancies are confirmed, the baby experiences positive affect, whereas disruption of expectations causes distress. Stern (1985) demonstrated this by asking mothers of 9-month-old infants to purposely respond with unexpected, mismatched facial expressions. Their babies became sober and eventually broke into tears. Winnicott emphasized the infant's dependence on the mother's facial responses in forming a sense of self: "When I look I am seen, so I exist. I can now afford to look and see" (quoted in Abram 1997, p. 214).

Infants who are cared for either in institutional settings or foster families are not likely to have the experience of interacting with caregivers who are able to provide the type of wholehearted, reliable, affective attunement necessary to provide predictable, empathic responses to their emotional cues. In many instances these babies are deprived of the consistent, day-in and day-out opportunity to participate in and learn the affective language of "mutual cueing" (Mahler et al. 1975, p. 49). These everyday, ordinary, affective interactions around feeding, bathing, diapering, playing, mutual gaze, soothing, and so on provide the basis for the infant's gradual development of the symbolic internal representations of self and other (Stern 1985).

Based on their empirical studies of face-to-face play between mother and infant, Beebe and Lachmann (1988) propose that the infant's social capacity flowers at age 3 to 4 months. This time span coincides with what might be considered the peak of symbiosis. Stern (1985) suggests that the infant's core sense of self, and his working model of mother, develop during the period from age 2 to 6 months. He notes that gaze is a potent form of communication in this process. The infant can use it to regulate the level and amount of stimulation to which he is subjected. During the first few months of life mutual gaze with an empathic highly cathected partner provides important developmental experiences for the infant. Schore (1994) states, "The mother's facial expression stimulates and amplifies positive affect in the infant. This is communicated back to the mother and in this interactive system of reciprocal stimulation, both members of the dyad enter into a symbiotic state of heightened positive affect" (p. 71). Schore believes that this state of heightened positive affect promotes maturation of the limbic areas of the cerebral cortex that are involved in social and emotional communication.

Emde (1981) also stresses the role of positive affect in the infant's emotional and cognitive development. Again it is the emotional availability of an intimately involved caregiver that seems to be the most central feature in promoting emotional growth. This type of intimate relationship is seldom possible in an institutional setting. The parents of Tamika, a child adopted from a Greek orphanage at age 15 months, described how excited they were when she ran into their arms at their first meeting. Only later did they realize that she ran to everyone indiscriminately. Even after one year in her American home, she showed no special attachment to either parent. Tamika was a smiling, dark-eyed beauty, but, in the words of her adoptive mother, "Her smile doesn't mean anything. It has no depth—she just uses her looks to con people into giving her what she wants." Despite her alert appearance, Tamika was slow to develop speech and took little interest in the educational toys her parents bought for her. She had a very brief attention span, flitting from person to person, object to object, pausing only for a moment before she moved on. She ignored her parents' efforts to make emotional contact with her. It was clear that Tamika had no language, either verbal or nonverbal, to communicate about her emotional life.

Microanalysis of interactions captured on film show that under good circumstances, mothers and their infants live in a split-second world with each influencing the other in terms of tracking the partner's direction of affective engagement and communication. Winnicott (quoted in Abram 1997) describes part of the process of mutual interaction as follows, "In other words the mother is looking at the baby and what she looks like is related to what she sees there" (p. 214). Beebe and Lachmann (1988) found that "the patterns of regulation of this face-to-face exchange in the first 6 months predict cognitive and social development at one year" (p. 312). Babies who have been raised in foreign orphanages may lack the early mirroring experiences with a significant other that facilitate the neural networks essential to the structuring of positive presymbolic representations and expectations of being able to successfully impact on caregivers.

As Rowe and Frank point out, babies who have not experienced an empathically attuned, responsive caregiver develop a repertoire of defensive maneuvers. They may withdraw, react with rage to frustration, or shut down and give up on attempts to elicit responses from caregivers. The vignettes about Lily, Jenny, and Boris provide poignant illustrations of how derailment of the early caregiving relationship can adversely affect subsequent development. Lily at age 13 months clings anxiously, Jenny at 8 months can neither sit nor crawl, Boris at 24 months clings to the hood of his mother's parka and wants to spend a lot of time on his mother's lap cuddling like a baby.

Other observers of infants who have had less than optimal

stimulation describe gaze aversion; body aversion; limp, motionless states; and hypervigilant, overactive states (Brazelton et al. 1975, Fraiberg 1982, Stern 1985). In the instance of Tamika, described above, any attempt to engage her for more than a minute was met with gaze aversion, inappropriate laughter, and frantic activity. Beebe and Lachmann (1988) cite a growing literature "documenting that variations in early social interactions do make a difference in cognitive development and patterns of attachment during the first 2 years" (pp. 327–328). They suggest that expectancies of misattunement are stored as presymbolic representations that will guide later structuring of self and object and the structuring of the experience of self-with-object. The baby who has suffered traumatic separations or perfunctory caregiving in the first few months of life will have few positive presymbolic representations to use in building a relationship with his adoptive family. Rather, this baby may be listless and unresponsive to the overtures of the new parents or, as in Tamika's case, wary and rejecting. When her mother tried to hug her, she stiffened or squirmed uncomfortably.

THE PERILS OF THE PRACTICING SUBPHASE FOR THE INSECURELY ATTACHED PARENT–CHILD DYAD

Recent studies of the practicing subphase confirm its importance in the development of the infant's brain structures and affect regulatory system. Since the child now has the capacity to move away from his mother, social referencing becomes an important tool for the dyad in the regulation of affect and behavior. The child can engineer brief periods of separation and reunion. If there has been a good prior relationship with a caregiver, the affective experience is one of exuberance and intense pleasure. Schore (1994) emphasizes the importance of this intensely positive affective experience. "The practicing phase in which the infant truly becomes a behaviorally and socially dynamic organism represents a critical period for

the formation of enduring attachment bonds to the primary caregiver. The nature of the attachment to the mother influences all
later socioemotional transactions" (p. 98).

If the mother–infant dyad has not had the benefit of establishing an empathically attuned mutual cuing system during the
symbiotic period, so that they can read each other's verbal and
nonverbal signs and signals comfortably, the "emotional refueling"
(Mahler et al. 1975, p. 69) essential to the practicing subphase is
compromised, or may not occur.

> The lack of mutual cueing was evident in the relationship
> between Peter, adopted at age 16 months from an orphanage
> in Colombia, and his adoptive mother. At first she was
> delighted by his intrepid exploration of every space in the
> house, but soon his frequent mishaps caused her great con-
> cern. Peter climbed on to high tables, tried to scale the living
> room drapes, and showed no fear climbing the stairs. He never
> looked back at his mother, and even if hurt in the course of his
> frequent falls, he did not return to her for comforting. As she
> said ruefully, " I feel as though he is always running away from
> me. He has no interest in getting to know who I am, or letting
> me find out who he is." As Frank and Rowe note, "Because
> there is as yet no emotional relationship, the child has little
> motivation to return to these virtual strangers." Another
> possibility in Peter's case may have been the use of hypomanic
> activity as a defense against the loving overtures of his adoptive
> parents. He came from a large, understaffed orphanage where
> little individual attention could be provided. There were few
> toys and virtually no opportunity for relaxed, playful interac-
> tions. Physical contact took place mostly around toileting,
> bathing, and feeding. A premium was placed on efficiency.
> Peter was not accustomed to the affective intensity of the
> dyadic relationship his adoptive mother was trying to form
> with him. Her enthusiastic overtures made him anxious. One
> of the goals of treatment was to help his mother to approach

him more gradually and to express her empathic attunement with his discomfort. She was encouraged to use humor and gentle teasing to set a more relaxed tone to her physical overtures.

In my work with mother and Peter (at age 2 years and 3 months), it was essential to take a directive stance to prevent him from using defenses that made emotional engagement impossible. He totally ignored verbal interpretations or verbal interventions of any type. His tendency was to surround himself with toys in a corner, and to engage in solitary, silent play. Alternatively, he moved at great speed around the office, touching various objects, totally ignoring both me and his mother. Frequently, she or I had to hold him to slow his pace, or to protect the office. At these times I empathically acknowledged how anxious it made him for us to touch him and talk to him. Using the puppets, I introduced themes of connecting up with feelings and with people. I had the puppets talk to Peter's mother about how scared he felt about feelings, and about being hugged or kissed. I tried as best I could to put words to any nonverbal responses Peter made. All my interventions focused on the current relationship with me and with his mother. When he avoided eye contact or touch, I used paradoxical interventions blended with humor. For example, when he closed his eyes, I told him what a great job he was doing of resting his eyes that were tired of looking at me. When he gazed into space as though I did not exist, I jumped up and down in excitement and asked him what he was looking at way over there that was so interesting. I wanted to see it, too. Eventually he began to smile at my antics and then to watch me, and laughingly tell his mother, "She's silly!" Peter's parents used some of these playful interventions at home with considerable success.

Hughes (1997) describes therapy with poorly attached adopted children as follows, "With the therapist in control of the pace, themes, activities and emotional atmosphere of the session, the child will haltingly, guardedly, but with a great deal of emotion, find himself being drawn into a close relationship with another human being" (p. 56).

THE CHALLENGES OF RAPPROCHEMENT

As the case vignettes presented by Frank and Rowe illustrate, children who have not had a solid, reliable partner through the early stages of separation-individuation have difficulty negotiating the rapprochement subphase. In the instance of Peter (described above), there was no evidence that he was aware of increased separateness from his adoptive mother until after she had been able to establish some sense of closeness with him. During the first year in his adoptive family, if she took him to a friend's or relative's house, he took off to explore without a backward glance. He disappeared into upstairs rooms and did not respond to his mother's calls. Trips to the shopping mall were a nightmare because Peter darted off across the parking lot, or into any store that caught his attention. He approached strangers as if they were old friends, with no sign of anxiety. As his parents, in particular his mother, were successful in their efforts to woo Peter into physical and emotional closeness, a dramatic change occurred. He showed signs of apprehension about exploring new places, and began to check back visually with his mother's face before proceeding. At age 3 years, he whimpered for the first time when his mother went out and left him with his dad for a couple of hours. He cried when both parents went out leaving him with a familiar babysitter. His mother now complained that Peter was her "shadow." She could not even go to the bathroom without him. Whereas in the average 3-year-old shadowing would be a danger signal, for this child it was an indication of a newly developed libidinal investment in his mother. At age 2 years he had been impervious to the word *no*; a year later he was very sensitive to any prohibitions or indication of disapproval from his parents. As Frank and Rowe emphasize, it was important at this point to alert his parents to view this shift as progress rather than regression. Fortunately, both parents were able to remain emotionally available and resisted advice from well-meaning family to send their son to preschool to "help him grow up."

Peter's father played a very significant role during this time. He admirably fulfilled the four tasks of fatherhood as summarized by Akhtar (1995a).

(1) By being a protective, loving, and collaborative partner to the mother, the father facilitates and enhances her ability to devote herself to the child. (2) By offering himself as a relatively neutral, ego-oriented, new object during the rapprochement subphase of separation-individuation, the father provides the child with stability, a haven from conflict, and (in the case of a boy) an important measure of "disidentification" (Greenson 1968) from the mother. (3) By appearing on the evolving psychic horizon of the child as the romantic partner of the mother, the father helps consolidate the child's capacity to experience, bear, and benefit from the triangular familial relationship and the conflicts attendant upon it. (4) By presenting himself as an admirable model for identification to his son and by reflecting the budding femininity of his daughter with restrained repricocity, the father enriches his children's gender identity and gives direction to their later sexual object choices. [p. 77]

In instances where fathers were not as involved, mothers became very overwhelmed by the special, at times relentless, needs of their adopted children. In the case of Tamika, mentioned earlier, her father became disillusioned after several months with her difficult, demanding behavior. The child's rejection of his early overtures was too painful for him to endure. He retreated to long hours at his job and abandoned the role of parent almost completely. Tamika had no haven when mother became taxed beyond her endurance, and she responded to her father's distancing by ignoring him completely. In late adolescence she chose self-absorbed, uncaring, older men who exploited her sexually.

CULTURAL ISSUES IN THE ADOPTION OF FOREIGN-BORN CHILDREN

Foreign-born babies whose physical features and skin color are markedly different from their adoptive parents have their own particular set of difficulties not mentioned by Frank and Rowe. These children are immediately recognized as different, and as "not really belonging" to the adoptive family and the surrounding community. Not only do they have to master the conflicts inherent in being given up for adoption, but their identity formation is complicated by having to come to terms with different hair texture, facial features, and skin color. When parent and child look at each other, there is no hint of mutual recognition. Tamika, an olive-skinned child from Greece with curly black hair, was adopted by parents with fair complexions and light brown hair. When an unthinking friend asked her mother who Tamika looked like in the family, the little girl chimed in, "Molly, our dog." Molly was a black-haired terrier. At age 8, Tamika refused to attend holiday celebrations with extended family. She said she did not belong. In school she wrote a story about a gypsy baby stolen from her family and taken across the seas to a far country. Her favorite fairy stories were "Cinderella" and "The Ugly Duckling."

This child had great difficulty in adolescence, the phase of development when maturation of ethnocultural identity is critical (Levy-Warren 1996). She had developed what Mehta (1998) calls "compromised identity" (p. 134) marked by a sense of cultural alienation. Tamika's heightened ambivalence toward her adoptive parents frightened them, and her, because the attachment between them had always been very tenuous. She did not have solid, positive internal self- and object representations to sustain her during this phase of further separation and individuation. Her parents' angry, anxious attempts to control her punitively made her feel completely abandoned and helped to push her toward identification with an alienated peer group. She stopped going to school, began to use drugs with a group of older Latino adolescents, and was sexually promiscuous. Eventually her drug use led to stealing and she was incarcerated in juvenile detention centers many times. At this point her parents' long-standing fears that she would be like her biological mother, who was sexually promiscuous and used drugs during her pregnancy, were confirmed.

The not uncommon fantasy of the "bad seed," and a dread of the power of the past (Hartmann and Laird 1990) protected the parents' vulnerable narcissism, on the one hand, and prevented them from engaging fully in reparative therapy for Tamika, on the other. There was pathological splitting as well as a strong fatalistic attitude expressed in "She's walking in her mother's footsteps." As Brinich (1980) noted in his work with families of adopted children, "They unconsciously expected the child to repeat his biological parents' unhappy story and, in trying to prevent this outcome, sometimes succeeded in provoking that which they feared" (p. 51). While the failure of this adoption and of the therapy with Tamika's parents was undoubtedly multidetermined, one factor that contributed was my inexperience at the time (fifteen years ago) with the aggressive techniques necessary on the part of parents and therapist to undo the child's defensive nonattachment.

Peter (discussed earlier), adopted from Colombia, was slender, small in stature, and had light brown skin and almond-shaped, dark brown eyes. His adoptive mother was very fair, had a stocky build, and was of medium height. His adoptive father was over six feet tall and blonde with blue eyes. The family attracted the attention of strangers who sometimes asked, "Where did you get him?" Although irritated by these intrusions, Peter's family handled them well and made no attempt to deny his ethnic origin. They took Spanish classes with him, alternated attending their own church and a church with a large Latino congregation, and took family vacations to Mexico and South America. It was clear that they found pleasure and pride and had a lively interest in his cultural heritage. The extended family (grandparents and aunts and uncles) welcomed Peter and he had many opportunities to learn about his adoptive family's history, which extended back to the American Revolution.

In his play Peter took the role of many heroes from North America and from South America. He learned chess from his intellectually inclined father, and at age 7 years was on his way to becoming a talented soccer player. He wanted Mexico to win the World Cup. At school he was one of the most popular and scholastically successful children in his grade. When asked to draw his family tree, he constructed an intricate, detailed picture of his adoptive family and his biological family (the latter was very positive, but mostly imaginative, because few facts were known).

CONCLUSION

Adoption of foreign-born babies is a relatively recent phenomenon, and more careful study is needed to determine what parenting approaches best repair deficits or arrests in development and facilitate healthy psychological growth. The data presented by Frank and Rowe, based on two decades of experience with parent–child groups, constitute a useful beginning to our understanding. More in-depth study is needed of the impact on the foreign-born baby of being transplanted from one culture to another that is vastly different. Even babies fortunate enough to have had a favorable caregiving environment in the country of origin have to be helped to deal with the multiple losses inherent in the experience of immigration (Akhtar 1995b, Bonovitz and Ergas 1999). As yet, we have little data to illuminate how the fantasies of adoptive parents about their foreign-born baby affect their initial attachment, and subsequent empathic identifications or alienating disidentifications with their child. Differences in skin color and facial and other physical characteristics, and their impact on the foreign adopted child's identity formation and sense of belonging in the family and to the broader culture of the new country, warrant more attention.

REFERENCES

Abram, J. (1997). *The Language of Winnicott: A Dictionary and Guide to Understanding His Work*. Northvale, NJ: Jason Aronson.

Akhtar, S. (1995a). *Quest for Answers: A Primer of Understanding and Treating Severe Personality Disorders*. Northvale, NJ: Jason Aronson.

——— (1995b). A third individuation: immigration, identity, and the psychoanalytic process. *Journal of the American Psychoanalytic Association* 43:1051–1084.

Beebe, B. (1986) Mother-infant mutual influences and precursors of self and object representations. In *Empirical Studies of Psychoanalytic Theories*, vol. 2, ed. J. Masling, pp. 27–48. Hillsdale, NJ: Analytic Press.

Beebe, B., and Lachmann, F. (1988). The contribution of mother–infant mutual influence to the origins of self- and object representations. *Psychoanalytic Psychology* 5(4):305–337.

Bonovitz, J. (1998). Reflections of the self in the cultural looking glass. In *The Colors of Childhood: Separation-Individuation Across Cultural, Racial, and Ethnic Differences*, ed. S. Akhtar and S. Kramer, pp. 169–198. Northvale, NJ: Jason Aronson.

Bonovitz, J., and Ergas, R. (1999). The affective experience of the child immigrant. *Mind and Human Interaction* 10:15–25.

Brazelton, T. B., Kosloski, B., and Main, M. The origins of reciprocity: the early mother–infant interaction. In *The Effects of the Infant on the Caregiver*, ed. M. Lewis and M. A. Rosenbaum, pp. 49–76. New York: Plenum.

Brinich, P. M. (1980). Potential effects of adoption on self and object representation. *Psychoanalytic Study of the Child* 35:107–125. New Haven: Yale University Press.

Emde, R. (1981). The prerepresentational self and its affective core. *Psychoanalytic Study of the Child* 36:165–192. New Haven, CT: Yale University Press.

Fraiberg, S. (1982). Pathological defense in infancy. *Psychoanalytic Quarterly* 51:612–635.

Greenson, R. (1968). Dis-identifying from mother: its special importance for the boy. *International Journal of Psycho-Analysis* 49:370–374.

Grotstein, J. (1991). Nothingness, meaninglessness, chaos, and the black hole: self- and interactional regulation and the background presence of primary identification. *Contemporary Psychoanalysis* 27(1):1–36.

Hartmann, A., and Laird, J. (1990). Family treatment after adoption: common themes. In *The Psychology of Adoption*, ed. D. Brodzinsky and M. Schechter, pp. 221–239. New York: Oxford University Press.

Hofer, M. (1987). Early social relations: a psychobiologist's view. *Child Development* 58:633–647.

Hughes, D. (1997). *Facilitating Developmental Attachment: The Road to Emotional Recovery and Behavioral Change in Foster and Adopted Children.* Northvale, NJ: Jason Aronson.

Levy-Warren, M. (1996). *The Adolescent Journey: Development, Identity Formation, and Psychotherapy.* Northvale, NJ: Jason Aronson.

Mahler, M. S., Pine, F., and Bergman, A. (1975). *Psychological Birth of the Human Infant.* New York: Basic Books.

Mehta, P. (1998). The emergence, conflicts, and integration of the bicultural self. In *The Colors of Childhood: Separation-Individuation Across Cultural, Racial, and Ethnic Differences,* ed. S. Akhtar and S. Kramer, pp. 129–168. Northvale, NJ: Jason Aronson.

Schore, A. (1994). *Affect Regulation and the Origin of the Self.* Hillsdale, NJ: Lawrence Erlbaum.

Stern, D. (1983). The early development of schemas of the self, of other, and of the self with other. In *Reflections on Self Psychology,* ed. J. Lichtenberg and S. Kaplan, pp. 49–84. Hillsdale, NJ: Analytic Press.

——— (1985). *The Interpersonal World of the Infant.* New York: Basic Books.

——— (1995). *The Motherhood Constellation: A Unified View of Parent-Infant Psychotherapy.* New York: Basic Books.

Tronick, E. (1980). The primacy of social skills in infancy. In *The Exceptional Infant,* ed. D. B. Sawin, R. C. Hawkins, L. O. Walker, and J. H. Pentakoff, pp. 144–158. New York: Brunner/Mazel.

Winnicott, D. (1965). The theory of the parent–infant relationship. In *The Maturational Processes and the Facilitating Environment.* Madison, CT: International Universities Press.

6

ATTACHMENT THEORY IN THE LIGHT OF ADOPTION RESEARCH

Marshall D. Schechter, M.D.

My father was a Corinthian, Polybus,
my mother a Dorian, Merope.
At home
I rose to be a person of some pre-eminence,
until a strange thing happened, . . . a curious thing . . .
Though perhaps I took it to heart more than it deserved.
One day at table, a fellow who had been drinking deeply made bold to
    say I was not my father's son.
That hurt me, but for the time I suffered in silence
as well as I could.
The next day I approached my parents and asked them to tell me the
    truth.
They were bitterly angry,
and I was relieved.
Yet somehow the smart remained;
and a thing like that soon passes from hand to hand.
So, without my parents' knowledge, I went to Pythos;
but came back disappointed of any answer
to the question I ask, having heard instead a tale

of a horror and misery;
how I must marry my mother and become the parent of a misbegotten
    brood,
an offense to all mankind and kill my father.
At this I fled away, putting the stars
between me and Corinth, never to see home again,
that no such horror should ever come to pass.

Sophocles, *King Oedipus*

Freud chose adoption and its vicissitudes as a major example of how personality development could go awry. And since the publication of Freud's work, the Oedipus complex has been a central core of psychoanalytic theory.

After five years of practice (1948 to 1953), I was struck by the number of adopted children, adolescents, and adults who were referred to me during that period of time. The number of adoptees in the United States was not known then, but subsequently statistics have been forthcoming that suggest that in children under the age of 18 in the United States between 1 and 2 percent are adoptees. During that five-year period, 13 percent of my practice was with this population of individuals.

The diagnoses of the adopted and nonadopted population seemed at that time very much alike, but in subsequent review of all of the cases that I and many of my colleagues have accumulated, it appears that the diagnoses most present in the adopted population are related to attachment problems, personality disorders, and genetic disorders (in cases where we had been able to trace their family background [Schechter et al. 1964]). We found that of 40 adults and 120 children, approximately 90 percent of our subjects appearing in the mental health systems were placed before 6 months of age in their adoptive homes. This was, for us, a surprising finding because according to what we understood of psychoanalytic and attachment theory, formation of close intrapsychic bonds did not appear before 6 months of age, ultimately being seen at 8 months of age as "stranger anxiety." Those first 6 months of life, therefore, were considered preparatory bonding time, and if a child was placed before this time, the attachments were developed that would serve as securing personality development—a kind of immunizing against future personality problems. I realize the leap that I am making has many statistical faults as we are not involving large groups of adopted individuals nor are we looking at prevalence of incidence studies, but only within the group of individuals appearing in our respective practices compared with the control group of nonadopted psychiatric patients from UCLA outpatient departments.

I was aware of the works of Lorenz and Tinbergen (ethologists on imprinting and critical periods of attachment at that time). But the research then extant did not force this conclusion as applicable to the human infant. However, increasingly research with prenatal, perinatal, and immediately postnatal neonates within five minutes and within an hour of birth clearly demonstrated that prior to and immediately after birth, the healthy infant has functioning and operative sensory and motor systems. Of course, these portions of the central nervous system are immature, but that they are definitely functional is demonstrated in approach/avoidance behaviors, alertness, and learning. It is clear that all cranial nerves are functioning prebirth, as I will specifically detail later.

In the mutuality of mother and child, it is this constant exchange and interplay between child and caregiver, this type of symbiosis and synchrony, which I believe is the background of what John Bowlby (1969, 1973, 1980) and Mary Ainsworth (1973) reflect as attachment and bonding, but which, as I will illustrate, may indeed be evident much before Bowlby and Ainsworth felt it measurable.

Bowlby was certain that there was a great deal more to the relationships than just behavioral interplay, as he defined attachment as an enduring and affectional tie or bond, specific in its form-relating attachment behaviors to a continuation of that bond. Bonding according to Campbel's *Psychiatric Dictionary* (1981) is "an interaction, a mutual dependency, often used to refer to the mother−infant relationship before separation-individuation has been completed" (p. 99).

Bowlby appeared convinced that infants were initially capable of forming only one attachment bond, which then became the prototype for attachments to other people. Soliciting response from the caregiver (part of attachment behaviors), Bowlby noted neo-natal crying, sucking, clinging, and later smiling and babbling, and later still, crawling and walking. He noted the stimuli emanating from the adult encompassing the auditory, visual, tactile, and kinesthetic systems, which captured the infant's attention, helping to create the linkage between infant and caregiver. Bowlby quotes Rheingold (1961) as saying, "Careful probing with improved techniques almost always yields evidence of keener sensitivity than had been suspected" (p. 73). Ainsworth (1973) states that it may be that immediate post-partum contact with the baby favors bonding by facilitating sensitive maternal responsiveness to the infant's signals, thus facilitating a general behavior that helps the baby become securely attached.

It is to this end—data bringing together some current research and my coordinating thoughts regarding early evidence of the anlage, or beginning, of attachments—that I present this material. It was a surprise, as I indicated above, that when we did the UCLE study of 40 adults and 120 children so many infants had been placed within the first 6 weeks of life. Infants' early placement did not serve as a buffer against later emotional conflicts. John Sonne (1998) talks of the first trauma of adopted individuals as prenatal having lived in an "ambivalent intrauterine environment."

Over the years in reviewing individual cases in my practice and reading the pertinent literature, I have been impressed with the sense that the seeming increased numbers of adopted persons seeking mental health services would be connected to problems related to attachment and bonding during these beginning mo-ments of life and possibly going off in a skewed direction, subse-quently creating for some adoptees a nidus for symptom formation derived from internal conflicts. This impression was enhanced by the statements by adult adoptees whom Doris Bertocci and I interviewed for our chapter on the "Meaning of the Search" in *The Psychology of Adoption* (1990). Many of the adoptees' responses to our question of how they felt they fit in with the adoptive versus birth families (for those who searched and found them) suggested that many adoptees did not feel they fit in with their adoptive families in regard to humor, pace, interests, talents, worldviews, intellect, and circadian rhythms, and often did not look like their adoptive families (hair color, height, weight, eye color, skin, shape of face). However, when they were with their birth families the resemblances to birth parents and siblings were startling (Fig. 6–1).

Figure 6–1.
Photographs of an adoptee at age 26 (left) and her birth mother at age 27 (right).

Adoptees often will carry pictures of their birth families, noting the intensity of the physical resemblances. Besides these physical resemblances, adoptees and their birth mothers have similar gestures, facial expressions, and senses of humor. Thomas Bouchard (Bouchard and Propping 1993) confirmed these impressions in his studies of monozygotic and dizygotic twins after thirty or more years of separation in different adoptive homes. Thus, we see the importance of genetic contributions in the attachment process and the intrauterine effect on the fetus of maternal emotions, drugs, affect state, and so on.

Along with the genetic implications of similarities physically and emotionally and in interests, expressions, and gestures, contributions to the understanding of the infant's needs comes from studying the caregiver's temperament and constitution. The appreciation of an infant's needs are enhanced by and more likely met if the adult caregiver can intuitively feel what the child, particularly under stress, is experiencing. Intuition involves the ability to organize and integrate silently and with seeming effortlessness (i.e., preconsciously) many different observations made over time. The process arrives at understanding without conscious awareness of the immediate mental steps involved; thus, the knowledge acquired has a sudden, unexpected, and therefore surprising quality. Campbel (1981) relates intuition to empathic responses based on intuitive understanding.

I am suggesting that birth parents have built-in mechanisms for recognizing at an unconscious or preconscious level the reactions, needs, tensions, and responses of their children, and may be able to respond more rapidly and adequately to the biological infant pushing the attachment connections with an affinity not possible for adopted infants. Perhaps, therefore, some of the problem areas in the adoptees relative to attachment, which our UCLA group discerned, could relate to an early failure of attachment on a prenatal level. Cadoret (1990) suggests that there are a number of inheritable familial characteristics that have been tracked, among them, the group of disorders known as attention deficit disorder in which hyperactivity may play a significant role.

We also are aware of increasing genetic connections with a number of other disorders, including bipolar illnesses and schizophrenia. What could we expect from an infant with proclivities toward hyperactivity placed in a normally active or hypoactive adoptive home? The child's sleep–wake patterns will be out of synchrony with the familial pattern, setting up frustration and conflict, which are potential backgrounds for symptom formation. If, however, the infant is irritable and fussy, and has difficulty settling down, or is reared in a family, either adoptive or birth, that has experienced these problems in other members, the tendency will be to accept these temperamental behaviors as the norm, leaving no fertile field for subsequent symptom formation in the interplay between infant and attachment figures.

There are other biological complementarities that we know enhance the bonding process. There is a rise in the pregnant woman in the level of progesterone in the last 24 to 25 weeks of pregnancy, followed by a decline, and then a rise in estrogen paralleling other species' induction of maternal behaviors. John H. Kennell (1976) and Panksepp (1998) note this shift in hormonal behaviors before and during delivery.

Specifically, the brain hormone oxytocin has been found to play a role in initiating maternal behaviors and reducing depression. In mammals, oxytocin induces lactation and mediates milk ejection. Oxytocin is synthesized in the hypothalamus, which is part of the limbic system of the brain and considered to be the cerebral center of emotion and motivation. Oxytocin induces maternal behavior as well as connections to the pituitary gland, which initiates uterine contractions. In treating children, we need to know the maternal as well as child history of responses to stress and conditions that calmed the fetus, such as music or the parent's voice.

We are aware of the potential effects of illnesses, drugs, and emotional states on mothers during pregnancy and on the fetus. As an anecdote, a neighbor of mine was beginning her third trimester of pregnancy. She was a very slight woman, weighing less than 100 pounds and just 5 feet tall. We met one morning and I inquired as to her health and she told me of an experience she and her husband had had the previous night. It was the summertime and they had left their windows open. As they were sleeping, they became aware of a fluttering noise and then realized that a bat had flown into the bedroom. Even though intellectually our neighbor was aware of the myth of the bat digging its claws into her hair, she became immediately confused and frightened, throwing the blankets over her head and waiting for her husband to get the bat out of the still open window. During that time when she was under the blankets, the fetus became extraordinarily active, nearly kicking her out of the bed.

Placental boundaries do not inhibit the transfer of illnesses or drugs, such as German measles, Thalidomide, cocaine, and alcohol, from the mother to the embryo but also in reverse in erythroblastosis fetalis (hemolytic anemia of the fetus caused by transplacental transmission of maternally formed antibody).

> Rh incompatibility may develop when an Rh-negative woman is impregnated by an Rh-positive man and an Rh-positive fetus is conceived. RBCs [red blood cell counts] from the fetus cross the placenta and enter the mother's circulation throughout pregnancy (the greatest transfer is at delivery) and stimulate maternal antibody production against the Rh factor. The antibodies reach the fetus via the placenta and cause lysis or destruction of the fetal RBCs. The resulting anemia may be so profound that the fetus may die in utero. [Merck Manual 1987, pp. 1766–1767]

Myron A. Hofer (1997) notes that attachment is deeply rooted phylogenetically and widely distributed, containing mother–infant interaction that proceeds from attachments regulating diverse physiological and behavioral systems in the young and in the adult (e.g., lactation occurs with sucking behaviors). Mothers could induce behaviors in the offspring that had shaped their own behaviors, such as what is needed to protect oneself in cold climates by prolonged nursing, increased ambient temperature, and keeping the infant out of the cold.

This form of accelerated revolutionary change provides a biological analogue to cultural evolution in which acquired characteristics can be passed onto the young. . . . A delineation of this symbiosis at the biological level within the mother–infant interaction lends some support for the concept of symbiosis in early social relationships at the psychological level. Developmental psychologists sometimes ask themselves whether they are reading into their observations the exquisite synchrony and reciprocity that seems to characterize mother–infant play interactions in humans. We are, after all, prisoners of our own cultural baggage, adult perceptual predispositions which is in fantasies. . . . This intricate dance-like pattern of interactions is not only present in less highly evolved forms, but is also present in biological and simply behavioral systems. Humans may have a long evolutionary experience with these types of interactions and a genetic predisposition to establish them may be built into our own biological systems at the level of our own endocrine and neural networks as well as our own behavioral systems. [Hofer 1997]

Many of these intertwining neural connections have genetically determined roots that are evidenced in research related to the sense of smell. Schgaal (1986) states, "Genetic-related individuals share functional similarities of skin glands . . . and recognizable similarity in their odor signatures."

There has not been a good way of testing olfactory system functioning except by using garlic as an aversive stimulus. Mennella and Beauchamp (1991) conducted an experiment in which they fed pregnant women subjects in their last trimester a great deal of garlic. Upon birth, the infants were offered contact with not only their mothers who had eaten the increased amount of garlic, but also with others who had eaten garlic prior to the experiment, and with a control group of lactating women who had not increased the amount of garlic in their diet. To the researchers' amazement, every one of the infants born of the garlic-eating mothers turned to those who had the odor of garlic either in their sweat glands, their breasts, or even their breast milk. This demonstrated how active various systems, including the olfactory system, are intrauterinely, and the study increases our understanding of how early bonding and attachment take place. This research clearly has significance in terms of the adoptive situation, where the child placed at birth would feel a loss because the adoptive parents would not have the bodily odors or have experienced the various crises or calming responses that the birth mother had experienced.

This specific area of research highlights the importance of early attachment processes that occur intrauterinely. It helps us understand why children placed before the end of the six-week crucial period after birth still have major attachment/psychological problems.

Bonding and attachment begin intrauterinely and are influenced by what the mother and fetus simultaneously experience before birth. Their responses are stable and often fixed and need to be recognized and dealt with psychologically for there to be any change in the child's attachment behaviors. The human being is a creature of habit, and the repetition compulsion derives from the repeated similar experiences including those that occur intrauterinely. Therefore, as a means of gaining an acceptable environment for the child, there needs to be a very careful and detailed history from the birth mother, who can tell the adoption agency the stresses, the happy periods, and the problems and solutions encountered during the pregnancy. Then the adoptive parents can replicate these experiences, such as choice of music and calming maneuvers, which the child encountered intrauterinely.

The abstract of a paper written by Schneider and colleagues (1999) states,

Previous studies have found that stressful events during pregnancy can influence the developing fetus, resulting in attentional and neuro-motor problems. This prospective study examined whether periods of vulnerability exist for neuro-behavioral impairments associated with prenatal stress, using a non-human primate model.

Twenty-eight Rhesus monkey infants were born to mothers in three groups: (1) Early gestation stress involving mild psychological stress from gestational days 45–90, (2) Late gestational stress from days 90–145, and (3) undisturbed controls. Infants were separated from their mothers on days 4, 9, 15, and 22 (±) postpartum for growth and neural behavioral assessments. Results indicated that infants from the early gestation stress condition weighed less than infants from mothers stressed during mid-late gestation. Moreover, whereas both groups scored lower than measures of attention and neural motor maturity, early gestation stress was associated with more pronounced and more pervasive motor impairment than mid-late gestation stress. These results suggest sensitivity to prenatal stress effects peaks during early gestation, tapering off during mid-late gestation. Clarifying the period of greatest vulnerability the prenatal stress moves toward elucidating the underlying mechanism for prenatal stress effects and may lead to more successful intervention and/or prevention.

CONCLUSION

Bonding and attachment begin shortly after conception and are reinforced through the pregnancy by exchanges of all sorts between mother and embryo. Upon adoption, the infant is placed in a strange environment that differs—psychologically, nutritionally, in maternal responses to stress and/or pleasure—from the intrauterine experience. Attachment disorders in adoptees stem from the attachments formed intrauterinely and need to be recognized in the subsequent psychological treatment offered to child and parent.

This concept was clearly enunciated by Sir Thomas Brown in 1642: "And surely we are all out of the computation of our age, and every man is some months older than he bethinks him; for we live, move, have a being, and are subject to the actions and the elements, and the malice of diseases, in that other world, the truest microcosm, the womb of our mother."

REFERENCES

Ainsworth, M. D. S. (1973). The development of infant–mother attachment. In *Review of Child Development Research*, vol. 3, ed. B. M. Caldwell and H. N. Ricciuti. Chicago: University of Chicago Press.

Bouchard, T., and Propping, P., eds. (1993). *Twins as a Tool of Behavior Genetics: Report of the Dahlem Workshop on What Are the Mechanisms Moderating the Genetic and Environmental Determinants of Behavior?* New York: Wiley.

Bowlby, J. (1969). *Attachment and Loss*, Vol. 1: *Attachment*. New York: Basic Books.

——— (1973). *Attachment and Loss*, Vol. 2: *Separation*. New York: Basic Books.

——— (1980). *Attachment and Loss*, Vol. 3: *Loss*. New York: Basic Books.

Brown, T. (1642). *Religio Medici*, ed. J. J. Denonian. New York: Cambridge University Press, 1955.

Cadoret, R. J. (1990). Biologic perspectives of adoptee adjustments. In *The Psychology of Adoption*, ed. D. Brodzinsky and M. D. Schechter. New York: Oxford University Press.

Campbel, R. J. (1981). *Psychiatric Dictionary*, 5th ed. New York: Oxford University Press.

Hofer, M. A. (1997). Early social relationships: a psychologist's view. *Child Development* 58(3):633–647.

Kennell, J. H. (1976). Progress in the study of maternal behavior in animals in birth interaction and attachment. In *Maternal–Infant Bonding*, ed. M. H. Klaus and J. H. Kennell. St. Louis, MO: Mosby.

Mennella, J., and Beauchamp, G. (1991). Maternal diet alters the sensory qualities of human milk and the nursling's behavior. *Pediatrics* 88:737–744.

Merck Research Laboratories. (1972). *The Merck Manual of Medical Information*, 15th ed., ed. R. Berkow, M. Beers, and A. Fletcher. Whitehouse Station, NJ: Merck Research Laboratories.

Panksepp, J. (1998). The foundations of human and animal emotions. In *Affective Neuroscience*. New York: Oxford University Press.

Rheingold, H. M. (1961). The effect of environmental stimulation upon social and exploratory behaviour in the human infant. In *Determinants of Infant Behavior*, vol. 1, ed. B. M. Foss, pp. 68–73. London: Methuen.

Schaal, B. (1986). Presumed olfactory exchanges between mother and neonate in humans. In *Ethnology and Psychology*, ed. J. LeCamus and J. Cornier, p. 1.

Schechter, M., and Bertocci, D. (1990). Meaning of the search. In *The Psychology of Adoption*, ed. D. Brodzinsky and M. D. Schechter. New York: Oxford University Press.

Schechter, M., Carlson, P. V., Simmons, J. Q., and Work, H. H. (1964). Emotional problems in the adoptee. *Archives of General Psychiatry* 10:37–46.

Schneider, M. L., Roughton, E. C., Koehler, A. J., and Lubach, G. (1999). Growth and development following prenatal stress exposures in primates: an examination of ontogenetic vulnerability. *Child Development* 70(2):263–274.

Sonne, J. C. (1998). Psychoanalytic perspectives of adoption. *International Journal of Prenatal and Perinatal Psychology and Medicine* 10(3):295–311.

7

ATTACHMENT AND ITS VICISSITUDES:

Discussion of Schechter's Chapter "Attachment Theory in the Light of Adoption Research"

Ira Brenner, M.D.

Although I never had the chance to work directly with Dr. Mahler, I have felt her influence throughout my analytic training, and I have had the good fortune of studying extensively with one of her early collaborators, Judith Kestenberg. One area of my work with her (Kestenberg and Brenner 1996) focused on the effects of massive psychic trauma on the developing psyche of child survivors of the Holocaust. Many of these remarkable people, now in their late 50s, 60s, and early 70s, were sent away at various ages to live with non-Jewish families and to assume totally new identities. In our international interviewing project, which collected over 1,500 testimonies, we learned how these children adapted to traumatic separation, culture shock, and the daily threat of capture. Under these life-threatening conditions of genocidal persecution and war, making a distinction between foster care and adoption seemed a bit absurd, since there was so much uncertainty about everyone's fate. The biological parents may have had every intention of coming back, but were marked for extermination and unlikely to return after the war. Those who did return were not necessarily warmly greeted by these children, who had already been sent away once. They often refused to leave the relative safety of their new mother's arms, having made new attachments and not recognizing the ragged strangers who claimed to be their real parents. For child survivors who were reunited, and fortunate enough to have stable, supportive postwar experiences, their resiliency and ability to readjust and get back onto a developmental track was remarkable. Yet the need to remain in contact with or search out their adoptive parents once they themselves became parents has become a lifetime preoccupation for many of them. Such attachments are profound, and they attest not only to the importance of traumatic separation from one's earliest objects, but also to the plasticity of the young child (Bowlby 1969, 1973, 1980, 1984). For some, these temporary parents became the sought-after objects of reunion instead of the biological parents. For others, the search for their long-lost biological mothers who never returned have filled their adult lives with a global never-ending quest. Especially for those who were so young that they have forgotten their mother's face, the feeling of incompleteness is very palpable. With this background, I shall comment on Dr. Schechter's thought-provoking and challenging chapter.

ADOPTION AND ATTACHMENT: IS THERE LIFE BEFORE LIFE?

Adoption has been making the news in recent years. There has been much public awareness of the genetic factors in adopting babies from schizophrenic mothers (Belkin 1999), as well as of the environmental factors in adopting Eastern European babies (Talbot 1998), for example, from Romania, where abandoned babies suffered extreme neglect and deprivation. Such problems raise the question of the impact of nature versus nurture on the earliest phases of life. Dr. Schechter's central thesis is that early attachment occurs in utero for the fetus and that "birth parents have built-in mechanisms for recognizing at an unconscious or preconscious level the reactions, needs, tensions, and responses of their children, and may be able to respond more rapidly and adequately to the biological infant pushing the attachment connections with an affinity not possible for adopted infants" (p. 146 this volume).

To put this hypothesis in a historical context, first I will briefly review some theories and then I will present a vignette. The effects of both prenatal life and the birth experience were serious topics of inquiry to Freud and his early followers. Ferenczi (1913, 1933) believed that the experience of birth was "indelibly impressed upon the mind" (1933, p. 402) and that there is "a continuous regressive trend toward reestablishment of the intrauterine situation" (p. 380). He saw the oedipal wish as the psychological expression of this original tendency, a position developed further by Rank (1929), Fodor (1949, 1951), and Roheim (1952). Ferenczi (1913) noted,

> For what is omnipotence? The feeling that one has all one wants, and that one has nothing left to wish for. The fetus, however, could maintain this of itself, for it always has what is necessary for the satisfaction of its instincts, and so has nothing to wish for; it is without wants. . . . The traces of intra-uterine psychical processes do not remain without influence on the shaping of the psychical material produced after birth. The behavior of the child immediately after birth speaks for this "continuity of the mental processes." [pp. 219–220]

Otto Rank (1929), who broke with Freud over his beliefs that birth anxiety was the root of all anxiety and that birth trauma underlies all neurotic conflict, looked for evidence of these experiences in dreams. Fodor (1949, 1951) also studied dreams in search of fetal and birth memories. Postulating prenatal amnesia after birth, he too believed there was a continuity of mental life from intrauterine existence on. However, he describes the problem as

deciding whether the fear (birth trauma) is retrojected from the
higher levels of the mind to the prenatal formations, or whether
higher level fear experiences have actually mobilized deeply buried,
organismic memories . . . and, having associated with them re-
gressively, succeeded in forming a constellation of great disturbing
potentiality. [1949, p. 304]

While he considers a variation of Freud's (1895) notion of
deferred action, he prefers the idea of an "organismic memory,"
citing fetal distress due to hypoxia as the source of fear of suffo-
cation expressed in nightmares. Sadger (1941) was even more
revolutionary with his belief that memories of preconception
experiences as sperm and ova could emerge in analysis and therefore needed to be dealt with for there to be resolution of neurotic
conflict. Much less controversial were Klein (1923), Greenacre
(1945), and Winnicott (1949), who also were impressed with how
birth and early postnatal experiences created certain patterns that
left their unmistakable impression on the child's development and
subsequent personality. Although Fairbairn (1952) did not dwell
on this area in his writings, he, too, believed in the importance of
the intrauterine experience, and saw the stresses of birth as the
prototype of separation anxiety. Paula Heimann (1958) and Wil-
fred Bion (1979) also speculated on unconscious memory traces of
fetal life. So we can see that there is a long analytic tradition of belief
in the enduring effects of our watery prehistory and first days on dry
land. In Freud's words, "There is much more continuity between
intra-uterine life and the earliest infancy than the Caesura of the act
of birth would have us believe" (1926, p. 138). But, there has been
a decline in the influence of analytic thinking on the understanding
of human behavior, and many classical ideas have been discarded.
    In the April 1999 issue of the *American Journal of Psychiatry*,
there was a challenging and controversial article entitled "Biology
and the Future of Psychoanalysis: A New Intellectual Framework
for Psychiatry Revisited." In it, Eric Kandel (1999) of Columbia
University argues that this decline occurred because psychoanalysis

did not progress scientifically or find ways of proving the basis of its underlying ideas about mental functioning. He suggests that analysis "might reenergize itself, and that is by developing a closer relationship with biology in general and cognitive neuroscience in particular" (p. 505).

The field of child development has been at the forefront of this movement, and I can think of no area more at the interface of psychology and biology than the perinatal period of life. I believe that more research is needed to determine if Dr. Schechter's hypothesis is correct, but advances in our technology already have made it possible to recognize the neonate's perceptual capabilities, despite the stimulus barrier. Indeed, Dr. Schechter bolsters his argument by drawing on the work of a number of contemporary researchers such as Mennella and Beauchamp, who document the importance of the olfactory sense in neonatal attachment. I'd also like to mention Mancia's (1990) study of REM sleep in the fetus, thought to demonstrate evidence of sensory integration and receptivity to psychological transmission of the mother's "internal representations" (p. 353), as well as Piontelli's (1987, 1988, 1989) research using ultrasound to demonstrate the continuity of behavior and responsiveness to stimuli before and after birth. Share (1994) has tried to integrate these findings, and in last year's Mahler Symposium on siblings, Parens (1999) asked, ". . . Would we go too far astray to propose that twins, in some precognitive reactive way, probably come to cathect their intrauterine cohort?" (p. 61). To what evolutionary advantage would this receptiveness be, if not to bond with the primary object? But even if this is so, perhaps it is still a bit premature to conclude that these earliest experiences form the template upon which all else is patterned. Furthermore, given the vicissitudes of child rearing during crucial phases, we know that birth mothers do not always do a better job than surrogates. After all, infanticide, postpartum depression, and postpartum psychosis would seem to be more in the domain of the biological mother. Nevertheless, these are most intriguing questions about the lifelong attachment between mother and child, and some of these questions may be best studied in perinatal adoption cases, especially in those situations where mother and child reunited in the child's adulthood. Analysts have always appreciated the importance of the individual case history, where the details emerge as the transference unfolds. So I offer a vignette of what may have been an uncanny communication between a very disturbed woman and her biological mother. This is a poignant clinical example of disturbed attachment and longing for the lost object, which occurred during the intensive treatment of an adopted woman who had been severely sexually abused by her adoptive older brother.

THE CASE OF PHYLLIS

Phyllis, a functional woman, was referred to me for treatment. She had an extensive psychiatric history that included numerous hospitalizations, psychotropic drugs of all classes, and electroconvulsive therapy. Yet in spite of all of these efforts, Phyllis would lapse into periodic depressions related to the frequent and unnecessary uprootings of her life. She would become extremely suicidal, after which she would mysteriously recover and then break off treatment.

Phyllis was rather avoidant in our early meetings. She was wary when I recommended regular psychotherapy in addition to her antidepressants, and did her best to sabotage my efforts to cultivate a therapeutic alliance. All she wanted was infrequent "med checks." She constantly questioned the legitimacy of psychiatry, as though it were the bastard child of medicine. Perhaps as a reflection of her own profound feeling of not being legitimate or belonging anywhere, Phyllis grew up with an exquisite awareness of her status. Any disobedience or failure to comply with her adoptive mother's insistence upon perfect table manners and a spotless appearance provoked a deep fear that she would be sent away. Phyllis bore no resemblance to her parents. Her swarthy complexion and tall stature made her look like she did not fit in with them, reinforcing her feeling of not belonging. She was regularly reminded of being adopted and what a privilege it was for her to be living with such a wonderful family.

Unfortunately, there was a great discrepancy between her parents' words and their actions, as was painfully revealed over time. Apparently, her parents were socially prominent and well-to-do, but drank excessively and never held their daughter, relegating such activities to the hired help. The teenaged brother showed more of an interest in her, but only for his own sexual pleasure. Memories of painful penetration at night, blood- and semen-soaked pajamas, as well as constant threats of exile for disobedience or for revealing their incestuous secret eventually came to the fore in defensive altered states of consciousness. A "dissociative character" (Brenner 1994) was then diagnosed, which explained much of the clinical picture.

At times in therapy, the patient regressed into such childlike states that her whole demeanor seemed transformed. She would become wide-eyed and vigorously suck her thumb, removing it just long enough to speak in short, clipped sentences characteristic of a 4-year-old. In this state, for which Phyllis had amnesia afterward, the patient insisted her name was Charity and wanted to sit at my feet. She loved to draw with crayons and would usually start with a cheery scene that was quickly replaced by one in which a malevolent figure like a monster would attack a little girl lying on a bed. Charity would then start to cry inconsolably until Phyllis "returned," often feeling embarrassed and humiliated by finding herself sitting in the corner with tears streaming down her face and her thumb in her mouth. She would quickly wipe her face and reapply her makeup, too appalled to inquire about what had just transpired. In this dissociated state of mind, the patient expressed a dependent preoedipal transference, professing a wish to never leave me and vehemently protesting weekend vacation and breaks. I cannot elaborate here on the modifications of analytic technique I have found useful in working with such patients with dissociative psychopathology except to mention several points: (1) the switching to different personifications is dynamically determined; (2) intrapsychic conflict is experienced as an internalized interpersonal conflict; and (3) this defensive constellation is designed to disown intolerable affects, drives, and memories (Brenner 2000). As time went on, Charity begged me to adopt her and to become her new father. In her mind, it could and should really happen! In her inimitable way of expressing the wisdom of her adult self in the form of this little girl personification, Charity described how her biological parents did not want her, how her adopted family neglected or abused her, and how finally she found her ideal new father in the transference.

We had been meeting five times a week for about three years when she decided to make me her storybook reader. She would sob incessantly at the end of each session, and she insisted that the only thing that would calm her down would be if I were to read her a story. Speaking in the third person, the patient said that Phyllis had just bought a special book for her, and would I please read it to her? I pondered the technical dilemma of responding to such a request, weighing the implications of being subtly seduced by this "youngster" versus wondering whether a refusal could ever be analyzed by such a damaged individual whose sense of belonging was so tenuous. I discussed my concerns with the patient, who in her current state of mind was not the least bit interested in these technical matters, and as she braced herself for her latest rejection, I felt heartbroken for her. Her mood brightened immediately when I then told her that I would consider it if we could talk about it afterward.

The patient quickly reached into her all-purpose bag filled with stuffed animals and very carefully handed me her new prized possession, a beautifully illustrated book about a young girl who was sent away by her mother to hide in the forest because of a war. There she met an old man with a beard who sat in his chair all day long in a little room in his little house, keeping her busy with chores. When the little girl returned, after what she thought was only several days, everything had changed and her mother was very old. The little girl was actually away for decades and had totally lost track of time. A guardian spirit had protected her the whole time, and she remained a young girl, untouched by the passage of time. After the loving reunion between the old mother and her long-lost daughter, they died in their sleep peacefully. This bittersweet story made little Charity cry with longing, relief, and great sadness as she drank in every word of this fairy tale, with such an obvious personal message. It was very moving for me also, as I felt this troubled woman's desperate effort to master the multiple traumas of her life, through trying to relive a new childhood in the transference. I found myself telling Phyllis an interpretive fairy tale of why a loving mother had to send her child away for her own good. Joy and sadness filled the air, and I had the feeling that she wanted to crawl in my lap, hug me tight, and never let go.

I had never seen the patient so contented and relaxed, a rare mood for a woman so tormented by nightmares and hallucinations of the past that she was a chronic suicide risk. But, in her young child state, the patient, as "Charity," was too afraid of getting lost to leave the office, so Phyllis needed to be summoned in order to walk out the door. Without such an active intervention to help the patient temporarily defend against her profound separation anxiety, she could have stayed in her autohypnotic trance for many hours, only to return spontaneously in a very disoriented state, a major problem in an outpatient setting. This time, when the patient's usual state of mind was restored, the deep affects continued to be felt consciously, although there was amnesia for the content of our session. Eventually, Phyllis reluctantly left the office somewhat overwhelmed and puzzled. Neither of us knew what the next day's session would bring.

To put this session in context, I will mention that about two weeks before, the patient had lacerated an artery in a more serious than usual attempt to purge herself of badness, acting on her quasi-delusional belief that she was full of contaminated blood. Without rapid treatment, she might have bled to death. This deep wound was still bandaged when the patient arrived for the session in which I read the book to her. The next day, in the midst of her associations, a violent transformation occurred. Suddenly, her voice changed and she jumped up off the couch in a rage, glaring and screaming at me as she tore at her bandage trying to reopen the wound. It was an alter personality I did not know, which meant that my alliance with the patient did not extend to this heretofore unknown autohypnotic state of mind. Phyllis started banging with her fist on a window threatening to break the glass and use a shard to either cut herself open again or attack me. She was not amenable to any verbal intervention and I sensed personal danger were I to try to approach and stop her. I told her that the seriousness of her behavior would require me to call hospital security if it continued, and she cursed me out with a vitriolic diatribe of obscenities, mockingly predicting that they would arrive too late to help. But I did call, and I told her that I was going out in the hallway, instinctively hoping that the physical distance would defuse her rage. I also knew that the glass was really plexiglass, so it was unbreakable. Although there were certainly other things she could have hurt herself with, I felt it was best to exit and talk to her from the hallway. At the time, I was too stunned to fully realize the significance of my intuitive response to give her space, and in time security did arrive, physically escorting her to the admissions office.

By the time she was on the inpatient unit, little Charity had reemerged spontaneously, but was confused and terrified by the uniformed guards, pathetically asking if she had been arrested for doing something wrong. With tears streaming down her cheeks, this little girl self cried over being put in "jail" (the hospital). Feeling somewhat shaken by the patient's behavior in my office, I had a lapse in empathy. I was gruff and I said to her rather curtly, "Just sign in! I can't talk to you any further about it now. We'll talk tomorrow."

Needless to say, these most unusual events gave me much to reflect upon before our next session. Indeed, I could not get them out of my head, and I was flooded with recurrent images of every detail, reliving them in slow motion, as I had apparently been a bit traumatized by the experience. As my experience with the psycho-analytically informed treatment of such patients with severe disso-ciative psychopathology was growing, it was becoming evident that inducing a sense of helplessness in myself through projective identification created an important crisis in the therapy (Amati-Mehler 1998) that signaled a deepening of the process. In this case, exploration over the succeeding weeks indeed revealed that her violent outburst was a reaction to the intolerable feelings of closeness and longing in the transference when I had read the story the day before.

Enacting a dissociated rapprochement-type transference (Mahler et al. 1975) in her childlike amnestic state, Phyllis clung and could not let go on one day, while on the next she tried to scare me away, actually inducing me to walk out of the office in an effort to defuse her rage. Then, when I had her admitted to the hospital, it was perceived as her worst fear come true: being sent away by her parents for being bad but not really knowing why. Underneath that fear was perhaps the imprint of being uprooted and sent away by her mother within days of her birth. The intensity of her separation anxiety and abandonment fears, coupled with the fluctuating na-ture of her attachment, more consistent with the disorganized/disoriented pattern (Main and Solomon 1990) described in patients with dissociative disorders (Barach 1991, Blizzard 1997, Blizzard and Bluhm 1994, Howell 1997, Liotti 1992) was graphically evident during this juncture in treatment. It became a paradigm in the treatment process, the reverberation of which continued for many years until there was neutralization of her aggression, coales-cence of her alter personalities, and the acquisition of object constancy. Rereading the fairy-tale was a regular part of treatment, which helped her work through the trauma of her adoption, and give her birth mother another chance.

One of the biggest secrets she kept from me was the discovery of her biological mother, which occurred before she started treat-ment; establishing a relationship with her biological mother was an enormously painful challenge that did not occur until after therapy was well under way. Interestingly, both mother and child contacted the adoption agency at the same time looking to find the other. For Phyllis, this fact had almost mystical importance, as though it were beyond coincidence or synchronicity and more of a telepathic connection. She was convinced they would not have reunited were it not for this co-occurrence, because the records had been lost. Phyllis was then given information and met her mother only briefly, prior to therapy, because a huge gulf of sadness, hurt, confusion, anxiety, and anger prevented anything more. But as her longing for belonging intensified in the transference, she mustered up the courage to give it another try. They began by writing letters, then speaking on the telephone every couple of weeks, and finally planning another visit. This time, Phyllis was much clearer in her mind about the circumstances of her conception and birth out of wedlock to a young woman whose boyfriend refused to marry her. The young woman refused to abort. Arrangements were made with an agency to give the baby up for adoption at birth to a couple who could properly care for her. Under the circumstances, the young mother thought she did the best she could for her daughter, but never got over the loss. She never married, never had children, and tried not to think about how it might have been. She was horrified to discover the daughter's fate and subsequent mental problems resulting from severe early trauma. Because of Phyllis's embarrassing symptoms, she asked me to speak to her mother, and thus once again I was asked to do something unusual in this case. This time I complied without hesitation.

Speaking to her mother over the telephone, I heard the same tone and melodic quality that Phyllis's voice had, and in her photos I saw an older version of the same face. There was no doubt that they were related. I shared in Phyllis's excitement over having reestablished contact with her mother, as her desperate need to feel that she truly belonged to someone was an ever-present theme in the transference that could not be analyzed away. I felt good about my expanded role as a facilitator, helping explain to her mother the nature of her malady that suddenly would transform her into seemingly different people—a desperate child wanting to be held and then an angry intimidating older self wanting to have nothing to do with her. Similarly, I helped Phyllis process her fears, resentments, and longings for her true mother, who swore she would never give her up ever again. This fairy-tale reunion was rocky, and it was practiced over and over until the two strangers who looked so much alike and seemingly had an uncanny communication became more comfortable with each other. The reunion was an essential part of an extensive and complex treatment, which ultimately enabled Phyllis to own her past and develop a sense of unity in her mind.

CONCLUSION

Phyllis and her mother appeared to have a connection with each other, the nature of which was multidetermined and not easily defined. The extent to which intrauterine and perinatal bonding left a lifelong imprint on Phyllis and the extent to which successive influences may augment or overshadow such a primordial experience have enormous implications for problems of attachment in adoption. Clearly, more research and clinical reports are needed to study these issues.

REFERENCES

Akhtar, S. (1996). "Someday . . ." and "if only . . ." fantasies. *Journal of the American Psychoanalytic Association* 44:723–753.

Amati-Mehler, J. (1998). *Crisis in the analytic setting*. Paper presented at the Philadelphia Psychoanalytic Society, December.

Barach, P. M. (1991). Multiple personality disorder as an attachment disorder. *Dissociation*, 4:117–123.

Belkin, L. (1999). What the Jumans didn't know about Michael. *New York Times Magazine*, March 14, pp. 42–49.

Bion, W. R. (1979). *A Memoir of the Future, Book Three*. Perthshire. Scotland: Clunie.

Blizzard, R. A. (1997). The origins of dissociative identity disorder from an object relations and attachment perspective. *Dissociation* 10:223–229.

Blizzard, R.A., and Bluhm, A. M. (1994). Attachment to the abuser: integrating object-relations and trauma theories in treatment of abuse survivors. *Psychotherapy* 31:383–390.

Bowlby, J. (1969). *Attachment and Loss*, Vol. 1: *Attachment*. New York: Basic Books.

——— (1973). *Attachment and Loss*, Vol. 2: *Separation*. New York: Basic Books.

——— (1980). *Attachment and Loss*, Vol. 3. *Loss*. New York: Basic Books.

——— (1984). Violence in the family as a disorder of the attachment and caregiving systems. *American Journal of Psychoanalysis* 44:9–27.

Brenner, I. (1994). The dissociative character: a reconsideration of "multiple personality." *Journal of the American Psychoanalytic Association* 42:819–846.

——— (2000). *Incest, Injury, Insight and Integration: Studies in Dissociated Trauma*. Madison, CT: International Universities Press.

Fairbairn, W. R. D. (1952). *Psychoanalytic Studies of the Personality*. London: Routledge & Kegan Paul.

Ferenczi, S. (1913). Stages in the development of the sense of reality. In *First Contributions to Psycho-Analysis*, pp. 213–239. New York: Brunner/Mazel.

——— (1933). Thalassa: a theory of genitality. *Psychoanalytic Quarterly* 2:361–403.

Fodor, N. (1949). *The Search for the Beloved*. New York: Hermitage.

——— (1951). *New Approaches to Dream Interpretation*. New York: Citadel.

Freud, S. (1895). Project for a scientific psychology, part II. *Standard Edition* 1:347–359.

Greenacre, P. (1945). The biological economy of birth. In *Trauma, Growth, and Personality*, pp. 3–26. New York: International Universities Press, 1952.

Howell, E. F. (1997). Desperately seeking attachment: a psychoanalytic reframing of the harsh superego. *Dissociation* 10:230–239.

Kandel, E. R. (1999). Biology and the future of psychoanalysis: a new intellectual framework for psychiatry revisited. *American Journal of Psychiatry* 156:505–524.

Kestenberg, J. S., and Brenner, I. (1996). *The Last Witness: The Child Survivor of the Holocaust*. Washington, DC: American Psychiatric Press.

Klein, M. (1923). Early analysis. In *Love, Guilt, and Reparation, and Other Works, 1921–1945*, pp. 77–105. New York: Delacorte.

Liotti, G. (1992). Disorganized/disoriented attachment in the etiology of dissociative disorders. *Dissociation* 5:196–204.

Mahler, M., Pine, F., and Bergman, A. (1975). *The Psychological Birth of the Human Infant*. New York: Basic Books.

Main, M., and Solomon, J. (1990). Procedures for identifying infants as disorganized/disoriented during the Ainsworth Strange Situation. In *Attachment in the Preschool Years: Theory, Research, and Intervention*, ed. M. Greenberg, D. Cicchetti, and N. Cummings, pp. 121–160. Chicago: University of Chicago Press.

Mancia, M. (1990). *The Diencephalon and Sleep*. New York: Raven.

Parens, H. (1999). Twins and other siblings. In *Brothers and Sisters*, ed. S. Akhtar and S. Kramer, pp. 53–68. Northvale, NJ: Jason Aronson.

Piontelli, A. (1987). Infant observation from before birth. *International Journal of Psycho-Analysis* 68:453–465.

———— (1988). Pre-natal life and birth reflected in the analysis of a psychotic girl at age two. *International Review of Psycho-Analysis* 15:73–86.

———— (1989). A study of twins before and after birth. *International Review of Psycho-Analysis* 16:413–428.

Rank, O. (1929). *The Trauma of Birth*. New York: Harcourt Brace.

Rheingold, H. M. (1961). The effect of environmental stimulation upon social and exploratory behaviour in the human infant. In *Determinants of Infant Behavior*, vol. 1, ed. B. M. Foss, pp. 68–73. London: Methuen.

Roheim, G. (1952). *Gates of the Dream*. New York: International Universities Press.

Sadger, J. (1941). A preliminary study of the psychic life of the fetus and the primary germ. *Psychoanalytic Review* 28:327–358.

Share, L. (1994). *If Someone Speaks, It Gets Lighter*. Hillsdale, NJ: Analytic Press.

Talbot, M. (1998). The disconnected. *New York Times Magazine*, May 24, pp. 24–54.

Winnicott, D. (1949). Birth memories, birth trauma, and anxiety. In *Through Paediatrics to Psychoanalysis*, pp. 174–193. New York: Basic Books, 1958.

8

ADOPTION, INSECURITY, AND FEAR OF ATTACHMENT: AN ILLUSTRATIVE PSYCHOANALYTIC CASE STUDY

Martin A. Silverman, M.D.

The developmental process is so complex and is fraught with so many pitfalls that Erik Erikson found himself wondering, as he stated in *Childhood and Society* (1950), how *any* child manages to grow up intact. If it is that difficult in ordinary circumstances, how much more difficult is it when the developmental process is burdened by additional complicating factors? Being adopted imposes such additional burdens upon a child.

If a child is to develop healthy self-esteem and self-regard, then that child needs to feel loved, cherished, and wanted by his or her parents and other significant family members. And feeling that way is a prerequisite for the child to be able to develop the capacity to love and cherish another human being. To love one's parents, it is necessary to feel loved by one's parents. For love toward one's parents to survive the feelings of anger and hatred toward them that inevitably arise in the course of daily life, it is necessary to feel secure that one will be loved by one's parents despite the upsurges of anger toward them that surface periodically. It is necessary to feel that the destructive force of rage will not sever the bonds of love that protect against the dangers of retaliation, withdrawal of love and affection, or outright abandonment. It is necessary to feel certain that one's anger will not destroy one's parents or drive them away. The capacity to hate, within a framework of safety, as Winnicott (1969) has pointed out, is predicated upon the stability and security of the bonds of love. This is the meaning, it seems to me, of the more or less universal desire for unconditional love, that is, to be loved totally, fully, and exclusively, even when one is enraged at and hates the person (originally the mother) from whom the loving is received.

Ambivalence, however, is universal in human relationships. People inevitably become frustrated and angry with one another. Children and parents are no exceptions. When the bonds of attachment are strong enough, the storms of rage between children and parents can be weathered, so that a loving relationship can prevail. When they are not strong enough, the hatred that erupts in response to disappointment, frustration, envy, intense rivalry, and other such negative states can exert a seriously disruptive effect upon the ability of a child to love her parents and vice versa.

Generativity and consanguinity promote the emergence and the maintenance of the bonds of attachment between parents and their children. Anyone who has had gerbils for pets and has mated them knows that the adult male must be kept away from the babies lest he kill them. And if the female is deprived of her sense of smell, she too will kill and eat them. It is the fact that they have come out from within her and therefore smell like her that protects them from the Medea-like ferocity that would otherwise emerge out of her genetic disposition to hunt and kill.

Human babies generally are desired and wanted. They also are endowed with characteristics, including cuteness and reflex smiling, that endear them to their parents. In addition, they carry their parents' combined and conjoined DNA, so that they embody the realizations of their parents' yearnings for immortality. Parents, relatives, and others almost universally express a keen interest in which parent the child most resembles. Rage and disaffection tend to be the immediate reaction of a man who discovers that the baby to whom his wife has given birth is not biologically his.

An adopted child is not fortunate enough to be protected by consanguinity from the disruptive effect of the rage reactions that inevitably emerge between parents and children.

> The impact is exemplified in the expressions of Bonnie, a 9-year-old adopted girl I treated some years ago. One day, she was playing with some little plastic animals in my playroom. She picked up a little cub that was somewhat ambiguous in its appearance. She puzzled over it. I asked what was the matter. She said, "I don't know if it belongs to the lion family or the tiger family." I looked at her and said, "You know how the little cub feels." Her eyes opened wide in amazed recognition. She case a piercing look at me and said, "Do you know what it's like to look into the mirror and not see the face that *should* be there?"
>
> She went on to tell me a story about a little girl who was adopted and about *how* she had come to be adopted. A woman was about to give birth to a baby. Her husband was ordered to go on a long business trip. She pleaded with him not to go, but he insisted on going because he didn't want to risk jeopardizing his career. The plane crashed and he was killed. When his wife received the news of his death, she promptly went into labor. There was no time to get to the hospital. Complications ensued, and she died in childbirth. The baby's birth thus was connected with the death of her parents. The baby, in essence, in the course of its having been born, had killed its parents. As Bonnie and I came to recognize as we worked together, it is the adopted child's rage at having been abandoned—and every adopted child starts out in life by having been abandoned—that makes her feel like a killer. And this is so no matter how much she is a loving child and feels like a loving child. Loss and abandonment are enormously painful, and difficult to get over.

When Bonnie was a little older, the focus of her short-story writing shifted to science fiction. It struck me that it was somewhat unusual for a girl to be interested in science fiction, a domain more usually inhabited by boys. When I shared this with her, she looked at me with apparent disdain for my ignorance and said, "I'm adopted; don't you know that all adopted children are aliens?"

In the course of human development we go through a much more complex and protracted attachment process than lower animals, who experience a brief and relatively simple automatic bonding experience. If a newly hatched duckling is exposed to a rubber ball rather than to its actual mother, it will bond for life to the ball rather than to its own species. Lorenz (1935) raised a little bird from the time it hatched out of its egg, and found that he could not convince it to ever leave him in favor of its own species. This was brought home to him painfully after the bird had matured into adulthood, when he felt a sharp pain in one of his ears one day. He put his finger in his ear and discovered that his little friend had tried to feed him some minced worm, although with confusion as to in which orifice to deposit the love offering.

The bonding process in animals occurs during a critical period, the length of which varies in different species. For sheep, it is just a few days. Sheep are widely recognized as animals that epitomize gregariousness. If a newborn lamb is separated from its mother for three or four days, however, it avoids the flock and is a "lone wolf" for the rest of its life.

Although human beings do not bond quickly, automatically, or in a relatively simple instinctive manner, there does appear to be a critical period, during the first year in particular and during the early years all together, in which attachment evolves out of the child's ongoing experience with a mothering person or persons. Fairbairn (1952), Winnicott (1965), Balint (1968), Bowlby (1969), Guntrip (1969), and other psychoanalytic investigators have explored this extensively. Interferences with the development of secure, loving attachment to mother, to parents, to family members, and onward, in a wave of progressive generalization, toward one's fellow human beings, one's special friends, and one's even more special love objects can wreak serious lifelong damage to a person's interpersonal relatedness.

Such damage is epitomized in the case of Daniel, a little boy who was brought for treatment at the age of 7 because he was not participating in his classroom at school, where he sat and daydreamed all day. Daniel told me that he didn't understand why people were so concerned. It was just that he thought about his mother as he sat in his seat in school. He thought about what she might be doing at the time, what they might do together when school let out, and so on. He acknowledged that it interfered with paying attention to classwork, but he couldn't understand why people were so concerned.

We worked together to find out why he could not turn his thoughts away from his mother to what was going on in the classroom. One day, Daniel and I were at the sink, making paper boats and floating them in water, something he had become quite interested in doing during his sessions. He was distressed that the boats kept getting so waterlogged that they sank. I wondered to myself if his preoccupation with boats and water had something to do with childbirth, perhaps the birth of his little sister. As we were speaking together about what we were doing, Daniel said something that conflicted with what his parents had said to me, and I told him so. "Those aren't my parents," he replied. "My parents died, and those people who say they are my parents came from Mars and took their place." He went on to say that he was only fooling me, but he had sounded serious and still sounded serious.

When I next saw Daniel's mother, I brought up the exchange I had had with Daniel. She immediately dissolved in tears. "There's something I haven't told you," she said. "After

Daniel was born, I developed a hot swelling in one of my breasts. It turned out to be a tubercular abscess. For the first six months of Daniel's life, I had to relate to him through a pane of glass. I couldn't hold him. I couldn't kiss him. I couldn't smell him. *We never bonded!* It was very different with our next one."

An adopted child has an even greater need than one who is not adopted to have the loving attachment between her and her parents nurtured, protected, and safeguarded against the disruptive effects of uncertainty, insecurity, and anger. What happens when circumstances complicate the adoptive process in such a way that uncertainty, insecurity, intense longing, and bitter, destructive rage over the experience of abandonment and loss are *heightened* rather than muted and minimized? In what follows, we shall meet a little girl who exemplifies the dilemmas such a person faces and travel along with her as she and her analyst struggle to resolve them.

CASE REPORT: JACQUELINE

Jacqueline was just 4 years old when her parents brought her for treatment. Her nursery school teachers had not merely urged her parents to obtain help for her; they had insisted upon it. She was being so defiant, oppositional, aggressive, and unruly that she was frustrating the teachers and alienating the other children. She would not pay attention, follow instructions, participate in group activities, or stay with the class during reading time with any degree of consistency. She grabbed other children's possessions but was reluctant to share her own things with them. She would demand that children play with her when she wanted them to, but at other times she would walk away from them or turn her back on them. She was distressed that children were increasingly indicating that they did not want to be with her, but she seemed unable to alter her behavior. It was all she could do to restrain herself from becoming physical with the other children to get them to play with her when they did not want to or when they refused to accede to her demands.

At home, things were not much better. She and her mother fought constantly because she would not obey, even though her mother's criticism was visibly painful to her, and, as with the children at school, she alternated between demanding her mother's attention and icily shutting her out. The last was especially hard on her mother, much more so than the terrible tantrums Jacqueline threw with some frequency when she did not get her way.

Jacqueline was extremely jealous of attention paid to her 2-year-old sister, whom she otherwise treated as though she did not exist. She alternated between coolness toward her father and interest in spending time with him when he was around (he worked long hours and often was away on business), but she was not really affectionate or loving with either parent. The person with whom she was most excited and loving was her grandmother, who lived a thousand miles away and whom she saw only twice a year.

Jacqueline's past history was very significant. She had been adopted in infancy through an adoption agency. Because of complications in the adoption process, mainly related to laws in the state from which she was adopted that presumably were designed to protect children placed for adoption, Jacqueline was placed in foster care for six months while the suitability of her prospective adoptive parents was investigated. According to what her parents were told, Jacqueline was a happy, thriving infant while she was with the warm, affectionate, attentive, somewhat older woman who cared for her during that time.

When she was removed from foster care and placed with her parents-to-be, she reacted in a way that alarmed them. Jacqueline was distraught. She would not eat. She would not sleep. She howled in seeming torment, and at first could not be consoled. This was distressing enough in its own right, but it also was alarming to Jacqueline's parents because, in accordance with the laws in the state in which Jacqueline had been born, the adoption would not become final until after a year of periodic visits to their home by a social work investigator whose reports as to whether they were proper parents hung over them like the sword of Damocles.

Jacqueline gradually recovered, at least on the surface, from her initial state of frantic misery, but her mother worried constantly, she said, about whether they would be allowed to finalize the adoption. With all the tension, the uncertainty, the difficulty getting to know and learn about each other, she told me tearfully, she and Jacqueline had "never truly bonded" with each other. She and Jacqueline's little sister, who was adopted at birth from a different state that did not require all these delays, in contrast had bonded easily to one another.

Jacqueline looked at me with a direct, steady, openly scrutinizing, but affectively blank face when I entered the waiting room to meet her for the first time. Her mother introduced me to her. Unlike most children her age, Jacqueline readily assented to leaving her mother to accompany me to the playroom. She presented as a sturdy, well-proportioned, solidly built little girl with strikingly observant, wide open eyes. Jacqueline began by exploring the playroom. Then she picked up a large, plastic truck and climbed under the table. She motioned to me to approach and, when I did so, shot the truck out at me. She motioned for me to return the truck to her so that she could repeat what she had just done. I commented on her apparent feeling that she had to protect herself from me, recounted briefly what her parents had told me about their reasons for asking me to help her, and said that I would wait until she felt comfortable enough to let me help her.

Jacqueline came out from under the table, looked up at me, and asked, "Do you know *Peter Pan?*" When I said that I was familiar with the story, she told me that she had seen the movie. She asked, "Can we play *Peter Pan?*"

For the next five or six months, we played out the story of Peter Pan. Jacqueline controlled the play. She set the scene each time, with quite good recall of where we had left off the previous time. She controlled the play, assigning the parts and deciding each time where we would start. Sometimes we would pick up where we had left off the time before. At other times, we would go back and redo a scene or scenes.

We started with Wendy and John, together with their dog Nana (Nana = nanny? foster mother?), leaving their parents behind in Boston (from where she had been adopted) and traveling to Never Never Land. She and I quietly played out this opening scene. In Never Never Land we met Peter Pan (which part Jacqueline always took from then on). Peter diffidently invited us to stay. John liked it in Never Never Land. He was eager to stay. Wendy was more cautious, however. She warned against our signing up permanently, preferring to keep open the possibility of returning to our parents in Boston if we decided to do so. On the other hand, she hesitantly agreed that having Nana with us probably made it all right to stay.

At first, Jacqueline maintained emotional distance from me. She showed no excitement or any real involvement with me. As producer-director as well as actor, she assigned parts for me to play and then treated me as though I were merely a faceless, meaningless journeyman sent to her by Actors' Equity to play bit parts. I commented after a while to Jacqueline that she did not seem very eager for us to get involved personally, to get too comfortable with one another. When I entered into the play a bit more exuberantly than she wanted me to, Jacqueline would look somewhat anxious. I let her know that I was willing to simply play the parts assigned to me in accordance with the director's instructions, if that were necessary.

There were sessions at times that started with Jacqueline, playing Nana, under the table. Nana would curl up to go to sleep, purportedly because it had been a long, tiring journey from Boston to Never Never Land. When I would step too close to the table, Nana would shoot the toy truck out at me to chase me away and punish me for disturbing her. I thought of Jacqueline's battles with her mother and her pushing her mother away from her. I thought about the difficult relationship between them of which Jacqueline's mother had complained, about the "lack of bonding," and about Jacqueline's mother's pain at seeing *her* mother getting a much better response from Jacqueline than she did. I thought of the wrenching removal from the foster mother. (I responded initially and in an ongoing fashion to Jacqueline's mother by actively joining with her in decrying the obtuse, heartless rules and proceedings of adoption that had interfered with the building of security and attachment between Jacqueline and her parents, as well as by working with her to help her feel more secure, less guilty, and more positive and optimistic about the ultimate outcome for Jacqueline and for them.)

I told Nana that it had been a long, complicated, difficult journey. (Nana seemed to me to represent one externalized aspect of Jacqueline's own self as well as her mother and foster mother, in a multidetermined fashion.) I said that I could understand Nana's caution about letting someone again approach her and that I could understand that she might not want to take a chance on letting herself get too close to someone and too used to someone and then maybe not seeing that person again. Nana calmed down and we were able to resume our performance of *Peter Pan*.

The themes that emerged in the *Peter Pan* play centered about (1) rivalrous envy of those who have a maternal caregiver, and (2) the intolerable pain of being rejected and unwanted. Captain Hook was enraged that Wendy and John had Nana. His rage increased as his efforts to cajole or steal Nana away met with defeat. The children would not give Nana up no matter what the entreaties or the threats were, and Nana would not leave them no matter what enticements were offered. I played the parts assigned to me, without protest and without embellishment, letting Jacqueline be in almost total control.

I expressed empathy at times, however, with what Captain Hook felt, that is, how *much* he yearned for Nana and how difficult it was for him to do without. I indicated how impressed I was with the children's unwillingness to give Nana up, with their loyalty to

her, and with Nana's loyalty to the children. I said that I knew how
hard it is for real children when people to whom they've become
attached are lost to them and I knew how hard it is for parents when
they love a child *so* very much and want the child to love them and
feel secure in the love between them only to have things happen
that interfere with all that.

Jacqueline had difficulty letting me completely express my
thoughts, but gradually, over time, she let me say more and more
until I could finally articulate the whole message. I noted how
difficult it was for her even to hear these things said. I could only
imagine, I said, how her *own* experiences in this regard must have
been. She responded by giving me a sharp but ambiguous look.

In the play, Tinker Bell tried and tried to get through to Peter
that she loved him and was devoted to him, that she would do
anything for him, but he repeatedly rejected her overtures. He was
only interested in fighting Red Indians and protecting the boys
from the Pirates who kept threatening to kidnap them. Poor
Tinker Bell pined away more and more until she was close to death.
(Along the way Jacqueline also had Wendy express hurt at her
brother's loosening his allegiance to her as his loving, nurturing,
maternal, big-sister protector and turning toward Peter in her
place.)

The fact that Jacqueline unfolded all of this to me gave me the
impression that she was beginning to be able to contemplate her
intense feelings about her losses and fear of further loss. I also was
acutely aware of how much pain her mother felt about being
rebuffed and pushed away by Jacqueline and how desperate and
impatient she felt about the situation. In her conversations with me,
she was sounding increasingly depressed and miserable, and she was
expressing increasing discouragement with what the analysis was
achieving. *Her* plight could not be ignored. I departed from my
stance of dutifully following Jacqueline's orders as the director of
the play. Now, speaking as the actor who was playing the part
(because I felt that she needed to reflect upon the pain she was
feeling and the pain she was inflicting, with the result that she and

her adoptive mother were growing further and further apart), I told Jacqueline, "I know you're the director and I'm only an actor who has to follow your direction, but it's so *hard* for me to play Tinker Bell that way. Her *heart* is breaking. She's *dying*. She loves Peter Pan and all she wants is for Peter to love her a little, and then she'd be so happy."

Jacqueline insisted that I play the part as directed. That was my job, she told me. "But I'm human," I said. "I *feel*. I'm not only an actor in the play but I'm also human. I can't *not* feel, as much as I might *try* to not feel" (an interpretation of the defensive nature of her hard-hearted lack of feeling for Tinker Bell, for her adoptive mother, for her little sister, for the other children in school, *and for me*, as she stonily insisted on having what she wanted rather than what she could have). So I said, with feeling (demonstrating as I did so that people could feel painful feelings without having to push them away), that I would try very hard to play the part as I was directed to do, but that Jacqueline would have to bear with me if I had difficulty doing it. I said I *felt* for Tinker Bell. Tinker Bell had feelings too. "*So do you!*" Jacqueline said, derisively, in a complaining voice.

I played the part as instructed. I had Tinker Bell pine away in hurt and pain and misery. But from time to time I expressed the difficulty I was having as an actor, playing it that way. I argued with Jacqueline periodically about the role. Tinker Bell was not asking for so much. All she was asking for was for Peter to let her love him. Did Tinker Bell really have to suffer that much? (i.e., did her mother have to be so utterly rejected, and could Jacqueline get over her fear and pain and narcissistic rage as a rejected, unwanted child enough to let her adoptive parents, especially her mother, into her heart?). Did Tinker Bell have to die? I asked.

Jacqueline implacably insisted that Tinker Bell had to pine away of unrequited love and die! But I was equally persistent. Maybe it did *not* have to end that way; maybe it did not have to go *that* far! Maybe Tinker Bell *could* live. Maybe she could be allowed to come close to dying, but be allowed finally, after all her prolonged suffering, to *live*. "How?" Jacqueline asked. "How could (*we*!!!) do that?" "How about Wendy?" I asked. Maybe Wendy, who was pretty tough and pretty strong, and very devoted to all the children in Never Never Land, including Peter Pan, could intervene. Maybe Wendy could talk to Tinker Bell and convince her to hold on and hold out and not give up but keep trying and keep insisting.

Reluctantly, and only after wrestling with it for a good while, Jacqueline agreed to let Tinker Bell live. She would *almost* die, but she would survive the suffering to which Peter was subjecting her. And then she agreed, with less adamant and less prolonged objection this time than she had made about letting Tinker Bell live, to let Wendy minister to Tinker Bell, nurse her back to health, and help her regain her will to live. Jacqueline was not so sure about restoring her to the will to *love*, however. When I expressed faith in the human spirit, Jacqueline responded, "Tinker Bell isn't human; she's a fairy! Don't you know that?" I replied, "Maybe fairies are part human." Jacqueline looked thoughtful when I said that.

Now the *Peter Pan* performance took a new turn. The focus shifted to Captain Hook (which part I had to play) trying more and more desperately, and with less and less patience, to convince Peter Pan to let him have Nana. After all, Captain Hook argued, Peter had Tinker Bell to look after him. Peter grunted: "Eh!" His tone of voice indicated that he didn't care about Tinker Bell. He also had Wendy to look after him, Captain Hook said. He could spare Nana. But Peter was unmovable. He didn't care about Captain Hook. He had no reason to give up Nana to him.

Captain Hook became outraged. He was inconsolable when his underling Smee tried to console him. He would get even! He would get revenge! If he couldn't have Nana, he would *kill* Nana! If he couldn't have Nana, neither would Peter Pan! So Captain Hook, with ever-mounting fury, set out to distract Peter so that he might get a chance to deprive Peter of Nana and deprive the children of Nana by *killing* Nana. I told Jacqueline that I was very impressed with how strongly Hook felt. He wanted Nana so very much, but he couldn't have her! And how infuriating it was to look on and see Nana with Peter and Wendy and John and all the boys in Never Never Land. He couldn't stand it. That must be what Jacqueline feels when she wants time with her teacher in school but her teacher is doing things with other children. And that must be what she feels when her mother is spending time with her little sister. "Don't talk about that," Jacqueline said. "Just play your part."

Captain Hook continued to pursue Nana. He was increasingly enraged at his inability to obtain her. He became determined to kill Nana. Jacqueline expected me to protest, as I had done about her having Tinker Bell die. "You're probably going to say Nana shouldn't die!" This time I went too far (indeed, I am human). I questioned, as an actor who also had feelings and was human, whether the story really did need that—but I also expressed empathy for the way Captain Hook felt. I could feel *his* pain, too. Captain Hook was a villain in the story, but he had feelings. (Jacqueline told me I didn't know very much if I could say *that!*)

Getting a little bit lost as I reeled amid all the murderous rage that swirled around me, I took a chance and ad libbed a line that had not been given to me: I had Smee ask Captain Hook if Nana really had to die. If Captain Hook didn't give up, eventually, just maybe, he *could* get at least some of what he wanted. Captain Hook's prompt response was to kill Smee, stabbing him with his hook and knocking him overboard. I responded with shock (quite genuine, as I had not anticipated this). Partially regaining my composure, I said, "Wow, I see now how strong Hook's hurt and anger are. He can't stand it. He can't hold it in. He *has* to hit! He *has* to hurt!" (I was thinking about her painful rejection of her teachers and of her peers and about her aggressive outbursts at school and at home.) I said that I didn't think Hook felt good about killing Smee, but I could understand how he felt and I could see why he had to do that *in the story*. Jacqueline threw me a quizzical look, but then returned quickly to her usual impassive manner.

Hook threw himself into his vengeful campaign with a passion. Wendy and the other children valued Nana enormously for her ability to protect them against the vengeful Pirates and Red Indians, whom the boys in Never Never Land had captured in an earlier segment and were about to tie up and burn to death, until I, as Wendy, intervened, asking, in sweet and compassionate, Wendy-like fashion, if their lives could be spared and they could be banished from Never Never Land instead of killed. Did Peter really have to kill off everyone who angered him?

Jacqueline did *not* like that. That was *not* my role, she said. I realized that she was right. I had become caught up in my own countertransference and in my concern that Jacqueline's parents might become so frustrated with the slow pace of the analysis that they might break it off. I had stepped out of my role as participant-observer in and patient, psychoanalytic commentator upon the dramatic expression of Jacqueline's emotional intensities and inner conflicts and had tried to manipulate her behavior. I apologized to Jacqueline for what I had done, and said that I had gotten swept up by what I had been feeling as I was playing my part and that it had seemed to me that Wendy, new to Never Never Land and from the real world, would feel for the Red Indians and not want them to die. The way she was in the story, she would be likely to implore Peter Pan to let them live if they promised to respect and obey him. Peter could magnanimously grant that wish to Wendy if he chose to.

Jacqueline surprised me by having Peter grant that wish. It turned out, however, that Peter was not being humane at all. What appealed to him was the opportunity to show Wendy *how little he cared about anything*. "I don't care," he told Wendy diffidently. "It doesn't matter." (This was a striking demonstration of Jacqueline's defense mechanism of *not feeling* in order to not care.) Peter banished the Red Indians from Never Never Land instead of killing them, though he warned them that if they defied him and tried to return, he would kill them in a gruesomely horrible fashion.

Wendy watched over Nana very carefully, keeping guard to prevent Hook from getting Nana. Jacqueline began to waver.

Should he kidnap Nana to have her for himself or should he kill Nana? (I took this as a sign that Jacqueline was holding on to the idea of reuniting with her lost, abandoning objects rather than breaking off all relations with them and destroying them in narcissistic hurt and rage.)

Hook set out on a plot to kill Peter Pan. Tinker Bell and Wendy, of course, rushed in to aid Peter, despite his scoffing insistence that he didn't need such (maternal and sisterly) help. The play raced excitedly and frighteningly toward its denouement. Hook obtained a bomb with which to kill Peter Pan, but the alligator, who had bitten off and ingested part of Hook—his arm—and wanted the rest of him, stalked him until he finally did Hook in, gruesomely and horribly. Then, in this version of the story, partly because I confused things by trying to slow things up so that I could keep track of what was going on, the bomb exploded, killing both Hook and the alligator along with him.

Now, it was time for Wendy and John to return home from Never Never Land. Jacqueline was edgy and fidgety. She did not let them return. She broke off the performance before they went back.

With the end of *Peter Pan*, Jacqueline decided to end our use of the playroom, at least for a time. We moved to my consulting room, where she became entranced with a large chair that swiveled. She had me spin her around and around until she grew dizzy and fell out of the chair. We played this game over and over. After a while, she added a new feature. She began to fall out of the chair "painfully," with difficulty, and to cry out, "You hurt me!" I said, after a while, "It's like you're being born."

Jacqueline said nothing, but she moved from the large chair to my chair by the telephone. She punched numbers at random. To her surprise, and mine, a woman answered. The woman spoke with Jacqueline for a minute or two. When she discovered that Jacqueline was calling from New Jersey, she burst out, "You better hang up quickly; I'm in Hawaii!"

Jacqueline and I mused together over her having reached a woman so far away. Encouraged by Jacqueline's calmness, I said, "I think you were looking for your first mother." She explained that when her family had moved to New Jersey two summers ago, she had had to leave all her friends behind, and she missed them.

We returned to the playroom and the play shifted to Jacqueline's making letters, with my assistance, to send to her friends. This went on for weeks. She more and more spoke of the replies she was eagerly awaiting. She was very sad that they never came. Finally, she had me make a letter arrive for her, although she had to have me do it in such a way that she could know but not know that I had made it appear rather than it having come for real.

Christmas was approaching, and her parents were planning to take her away with them for a vacation. She was distressed and disorganized by the prospect of leaving me. Jacqueline became preoccupied with the need to come up with a present for me. Finally, she brought in a penny (a reflection, perhaps, of how little value she placed on herself and her power?). She searched and searched uncertainly to find a safe place to put it. She made me promise that I would take care of it and make sure that it would not disappear. She wanted me to keep it in my pocket "always."

She agitatedly and indecisively struggled to figure out what she wanted from me for Christmas. She finally made up her mind. She came in with a Polaroid camera and took a picture of me. *That* was what she wanted.

When the day came for her to say good-bye before she left for Disney World, she was enraged. How could I part from her? Never mind that she was the one leaving me. How could I part from *her*? She became more and more agitated (still in the waiting room), leaned over, and bit a button off my jacket sleeve! Thinking of the alligator who had bitten off part of Captain Hook but wanted the rest of him, I said, "I think you want to eat me up so you can have me inside of you and take me with you." "Then you can *never* leave me," she replied. Her parents looked on in awe. (I subsequently spoke about this with them to help them understand more fully the role of transference as a temporary phenomenon in psychoanalytic work. Jacqueline's mother already felt hurt and rejected by the difficult, ambivalent behavior Jacqueline exhibited with her while she seemed to long instead for her idealized grandmother far away, and, presumably, for her idealized mother (s) of the past with whom her mother could not, in real life, compete. It would have been far too painful for her if she were to perceive Jacqueline's analyst as becoming yet another maternal rival for Jacqueline's affections.)

Jacqueline and I went into the playroom together and talked about what had happened. Her parents loved her, I said, and were taking her away with them for a wonderful Disney World vacation that they very much wanted her to enjoy together with them. Jacqueline acknowledged that she was looking forward to Disney World. "But it's so hard for you to be separated from a friend. It must feel like you'll lose me and never see me again. I think it reminds you too much of things that happened in the past that were very painful." She accepted the Christmas present I had prepared for her, a memory game, without any emotional expression. Having a game from me, to remember me by, was not enough. Loss was too unbearable for Jacqueline. She had to have me, not a substitute token for me.

To my surprise, I received a postcard from Florida, signed "LOVE, Jacqueline." When she returned, she immediately searched for the penny she had given me. She seemed glad to find it. But she informed me that she had lost the photograph of me which she had taken to Florida with her. She didn't know what had happened to it. Somehow it had disappeared.

Over the next six weeks, we spoke together about what had taken place around the vacation separation between us. Jacqueline's anxiety and pain over separation and loss, and her difficulty accepting a substitute for what she had lost, because of what she had experienced in the past, were the main topics. While we were talking (with periodic time out to play some games, a new development in the analysis), Jacqueline carefully and painstakingly, with great persistence and loving devotion, worked at making me an elaborate Valentine's Day card. It was replete with a big red heart and an elegant lace border that she carefully constructed with paper and scissors.

The day before Valentine's Day, the card appeared to be ready. When time came for Jacqueline to leave, however, she asked for just a little more time to put some final touches to it. Then she asked for a little more time, and yet a little more time. The next patient had arrived. I commented that it seemed to be very difficult for Jacqueline to leave. She kept feeling that she needed yet a little bit more of me. Maybe we'd be able to figure out what that was all about, but we did have to stop. Jacqueline erupted in fury. She grabbed up the Valentine's Day card and tore it into pieces! I was dumbfounded. "How could you do that?" I cried out. "You worked on that for weeks!" She stalked out.

Forty-five minutes later, the telephone rang. It was Jacqueline. "Hi." That was all she said. After a moment, I said "Hi." She said nothing. "How come you called?" I asked. "I just felt like," she replied. Then she was silent. I said, "Jacqueline, what happened? How could you tear up that card, after all the work you did on it?" "It doesn't matter." "It doesn't matter!" I said. "It does matter!" "It doesn't matter. It's only a card." Jacqueline paused.

Then she spoke. "Where are you?" I asked what she meant. "Just answer," she said. "I'm in my office, sitting by the phone." "What are you wearing?" "You know what I'm wearing," I said. "You just left here a little while ago." "What are you wearing?" Jacqueline had me describe my clothes, the room, what I saw out the window, and so on. I realized that Jacqueline needed to rebuild her mental photograph of me. I told her that it seemed to me that she had gotten so angry at me when I sent her away to see another child, even after she had made me that wonderful Valentine, that she not only ripped up the card she had made of me, but she also ripped up the picture she had of me inside her head. She'd been so angry at me for not staying with her that her anger destroyed her other feelings for me and, in a way, destroyed *me*.

I told her that I felt bad that she had torn up the card and that

I felt bad for her and for her pain. "It doesn't matter," she said. "The card's not important." "Yes it is," I said. "*You broke my heart!*"

We spent a lot of time talking about this incident in the months that followed. We analyzed it together in terms of her fear of getting close to me and letting me get close to her, in terms of her inability to share me with other children, in terms of her fear of loving me and of letting me love her, in terms of the pain of other children (and sometimes their parents) not liking her, in terms of the world being difficult in ways, and, in connection with all of this, in terms of the circumstances of her adoption and their impact upon her relationship with her parents.

I indicated to Jacqueline that, while I understood that the card was not important, as she had said, her *feelings* were important. I knew, I said, thinking back to the *Peter Pan* time, that it was not my job to have feelings in response to what she brought to me to help her with, but that I did have feelings nevertheless and that I could tolerate that. I pointed out to Jacqueline that she too had feelings, even though she wished she didn't sometimes, and I said to her that it seemed to me that she too could tolerate them. I invited her to face the feelings within her that were connected with the Valentine card incident. She agreed to talk with me about the incident.

We became able to analyze what had occurred. What emerged made it clear that Jacqueline had come to feel, as a result of our work together and, most acutely to her, in relation to what had transpired between us around the Christmas vacation trip that had taken her away from me, that I was very special to her and it was painful to her to lose me. Her feelings in connection with losing me when her parents took her away from me had stirred the feelings buried deep inside of her about the earlier losses, first of her original mother (her biological mother and her early foster mother combined), then of her friends when the family moved, and then of her current (adoptive) mother when her little sister was born and adopted into the family. The valentine card had represented a search for the idealized, wonderful, perfect, great mother who she felt was out there somewhere (like the woman in

Hawaii she had called from my office) and with whom she longed to be united. When I had sent her away so that I could see another child, I had dashed her hopes of finding that special mother through me and thrown her into a rage that had destroyed all possibility of loving me and having me as the embodiment of the fantasized object of her desperate longing. We also came to see the valentine card incident, and certain aspects of her way of relating to me (aloofness, coolness, pushing me away whenever she found herself drawn closer to me, etc.), as reflective of oedipal conflicts that plagued her.

While we talked, we played games or Jacqueline draw pictures. Interestingly, she also worked at constructing love notes to her mother, Mother's Day cards, Father's Day cards, and invitations to her maternal aunt's wedding, which was coming up. Now she was extending tendrils of love and affection toward her actual family members rather than toward a fantasized, idealized supermother whom she was insisting on having. She became able to speak with me about irritations and angers that flared up against her mother and sister rather than fight her mother and shoo away or ignore her sister. Her relationship with both of them improved, as did her behavior in school.

Jacqueline became interested in looking at herself in the mirror when she came to see me. She was less interested in using the big floor-to-ceiling mirror in the entrance hall, which she could use all by herself, than in using the little bathroom mirror. Since I had to hold her up for her to reach the bathroom mirror, she did not see only her face in that mirror when she looked into it but saw her face and mine together, or her face and part of my face, or my face and part of her face. She and I talked about this together in terms of her feelings about not looking like her parents or sister, because of the adoptions. It is my impression, however, that Jacqueline was also using the little bathroom and the little bathroom mirror to build a special place and togetherness with me and to develop a union with me through which she could work at building the capacity for union with an other as part of her self and vice versa, so that she could possess a self-as-part-of-other and feel the security of an other-as-part-of-self.

Along the way, Jacqueline's parents went away together on a trip to California. This was the first time she had been able to let them leave her. She came in for a session looking pale, drawn, and strained. She could barely relate to me. "You're thinking about your parents, aren't you?" I said. "I think about them all the time." "You miss them." "I miss them very much."

Jacqueline began to complain about being hungry. She complained more and more plaintively. The babysitter had forgotten to give her an after-school snack. How could she talk to me if she was so hungry that all she could think about was being hungry? As she spoke, she gently stroked the large breasts of an African art statue of a naked woman with a naked child on her back that she had picked up from my desk. She pleaded with me to give her something to eat (which I had never done before). She was becoming so agitated and distraught that I agreed to get something for her to eat.

I went out and brought back some strawberries and a tangerine. She ignored the strawberries, but wolfed down the tangerine. Then she sat, speaking dreamily to me and stroking the tangerine peel the way she had stroked the breasts of the sculpture from my desk. "You know what I think?" I said. "I think you'd like me to grow breasts and become a Mommy for you." "COULD YOU!?!" she exclaimed.

I said I wished it could be that simple. Her feelings with her Mommy were the important thing. I said that I couldn't replace her Mommy but we could feel together and talk together about all this so that I could help her deal with it better. She listened attentively. I said, "I think you're afraid they're not coming back. You're not *sure* of them—the way you weren't sure I'd still have the penny you gave me when you came back from Disney World that time. You're not sure they *want to* come back." "They said they *miss* me." "When?" "On the phone. Mommy and Daddy called on the phone." "But you're not *sure* they miss you. You're not *sure* they want to come back. You're afraid they're glad to be away without you, and you miss them." "They *said* they miss me." "But you think they miss Katey [her little sister] *more*." "They *do* miss Katey more," Jacqueline said. "She's *nice*." I said, "And you're not able to be nice." Jacqueline said, "They'll come back." I said, "But it's hard to wait." She responded, "It's very hard." I said, "I'll help you wait. I'll help you the best I can." She said, "I know."

Jacqueline's parents had to break off her treatment before Jacqueline and I had decided that it was time to stop. Apparently, now that Jacqueline's behavior had improved and she had begun to develop a truly loving bond to them, they needed her to give me up as her special friend and as alternative object of her affection so that she might develop an ever-deeper attachment to them, her adoptive parents with whom she had a lot of catching up to do. Still not entirely secure as her love objects, they most probably also needed to remove me from the scene as a rival for Jacqueline's affections. Perhaps they also had to redo the process of taking over from a "birth" mother and "foster" mother.

It took some effort on my part to convince Jacqueline's parents to let us have three months in which to wind things up and then part from one another on fond terms rather than breaking off the analysis abruptly. It was not an altogether easy three months either for Jacqueline or for me, but maybe that was how it had to be.

CONCLUSION

Jacqueline went through an adoption experience that greatly interfered with her ability to become securely and safely bonded with her mother. Her insecurity, the tenuousness and fragility of her attachment to her love objects, her fear of being rejected and hurt, her sensitivity to loss and potential loss, her inability to share love and affection, her difficulty accepting limitations in the satisfaction of her powerful hunger for total and exclusive unconditional love; and the disruptive effect of her eruptions of destructive rage

rendered her incapable of maintaining the kind of loving relationship with her parents and sister that would enable her to tolerate the
inevitable frustrations and minor losses that are part of real-world
experience. She clung instead to fantasies in which she either felt
nothing toward anyone and needed no one or she searched to
reunite with the idealized, all-perfect, unconditionally, totally and
exclusively loved and loving mother she had lost. She could accept
nothing in between.

During the opening phase of the analysis, Jacqueline expressed, via the story of Peter Pan, her reluctance to feel anything
toward anyone, her peremptory need to control her feelings and to
control her relationships with people, and her insistence on needing no one. When this was dealt with analytically, within the
context of our playing out the story, by addressing the defensive
nature of her stance, and demonstrating that feelings *could be*
tolerated and contended with, she was able to move on to revealing
the pain she felt at having undergone multiple losses and expressing
her yearning to be reunited with her lost objects.

When I demonstrated that I empathized with her pain and
with her fear of becoming attached to someone again, only to
undergo a repeat of the pain of abandonment and loss, Jacqueline
proceeded, via the valentine card incident, to demonstrate her
unwillingness to accept less than full and total realization of her
wish to be united with the idealized, perfect mother that appeared
to represent a core fantasy. Analysis of this transferential enactment
of the fantasy, together with my demonstration of willingness to
truly feel her pain and her sorrow and my willingness to be the
object of the rage she felt, permitted her to wrestle analytically with
her conflicted yearnings, recognize the futility of adamantly insisting upon total realization of her dream or nothing, make use of
symbolic substitutes for the first time, and turn to the love objects
who were available to her in real life for at least some of what she
wanted.

In the final phase of the analysis, Jacqueline was able to make
use of me to build up the sense of self joined with reliable other

that could facilitate her capacity to incur the risks involved in turning meaningfully and realistically to others as objects of her love and sources of love for her. Her relationships in the world at large improved, and she became able to give up her friend, the analyst, and move on without him. Her development was now on track. Analysis had enabled her to overcome the interferences that her early experiences had imposed upon her capacity to take risks, accept limitations, and love her parents and her sister. No longer would she have to be Peter Pan.

REFERENCES

Balint, M. (1968). *The Basic Fault*. London: Tavistock.

Bowlby, J. (1969). *Attachment and Loss*, Vol. 1: *Attachment*. London: Hogarth.

Erikson, E. H. (1950). *Childhood and Society*. New York: Norton.

Fairbairn, W. R. D. (1952). *Psychoanalytic Studies of the Personality*. London: Tavistock.

Guntrip, H. (1969). *Schizoid Phenomenon, Object Relations, and the Self*. New York: International Universities Press.

Lorenz, K. (1935). Companionship in bird life. In *Instinctive Behavior*, ed. C. H. Schiller, pp. 83–175. New York: International Universities Press, 1957.

Winnicott, D. W. (1965). *The Maturational Processes and the Facilitating Environment*. New York: International Universities Press.

———— (1969). The mother–infant experience of mutuality. In *Psychoanalytic Explorations: D. W. Winnicott*, ed. C. Winnicott, R. Shepherd, and M. Davis, pp. 251–260. Cambridge: Harvard University Press, 1989.

9

THE PAIN OF BROKEN BONDS

*Discussion of Silverman's Chapter
"Adoption, Insecurity, and
Fear of Attachment"*

Paul R. Viola, M.D.

It is a great pleasure and privilege to discuss Dr. Silverman's contribution because here is the sort of knowledge that only psychoanalysis provides, the knowledge of what transpires in the depths of the human heart, the heart of a very troubled young child. Feelings of rage and grief that can be the outcome of an adoption for both child and parents, can be approximated in other life experiences as well, to which many of us can relate. Personal insecurity, dependency and loss, the ambivalence of love and hate, and uncertainty of an existential degree challenge human beings in many situations and levels of development. As in other child analytic material, awareness of the role of the mother easily draws our attention, but often not the position and significance of fathers.

Deeply moving, in the case presented to us by Dr. Silverman, are the pain of rejection and the hostile narcissistic estrangement manifested by the child, Jacqueline. She was a cause of heartache and worry to her adoptive mother. (We know less of the impact of the care of this child upon the adoptive father.) She demanded attention or icily shut others out—other children in school, her younger sister, her adoptive parents, and finally Dr. Silverman. Yet he managed to engage with her in an analytic treatment, and raises those perennial questions: What was therapeutic in the process? What elements were particularly crucial? Why was the process interrupted prematurely?

A BRIEF DIGRESSION INTO THE LITERATURE

Wieder's (1977a,b) papers are a rich source of both case material and clear observations. He demonstrated that knowledge of adoption conveyed too early and injudiciously to a young child, even with the best of conscious intentions, can amount to a "forceful pathogen" in the child's mental life. As Peller (1961) had discussed, whatever is said by way of explanation to a prelatency child is likely to be "drawn into the whirlpool of the child's . . . fantasies, or will be promptly denied, pushed aside. The child is too enmeshed in his own fantasies, his powerful wishes and anxieties. Gross distortion, denial, or oblivion is the fate of *all* he hears or sees that *comes close to his vulnerable areas and to his own conflicts.* Information about adoption is bound to suffer the same fate" (p. 145).

Wieder's cases from childhood, adolescence, and adulthood showed the prevalence of fantasies of "being gotten rid of," perhaps for reasons of being shameful or bad; anal-stage imagery of debasement of the self; fantasies of being "cast out to die," then found and rescued by the adoptive mother; and the amplified anxiety and confusion when normal developmental threats of loss of the object and loss of love occur in the context of heightened actuality. It becomes much more difficult for the child to reconcile split representations of good and bad mother; denial more severely affects reality testing, cognitive functioning, and object relations; and an intensified sense of the probability of fantasies is common.

Brinich (1980) also states that the "realities of the adults mean *nothing* to the young child" (p. 125). Adoption, he says, occurs always in a context of pain, referring to the death of the birth parents or to their inability or unwillingness to care for the child, and to the adoptive parents' degree of sense of failure at not having been able to conceive. As the other authors confirm, the adopted child grows with an intrapsychic representational world compounded by two separate sets of parents. Unfortunately, the adopted child's genealogy by "others" offers opportunity for externalized blame of unacceptable drive behavior. In proportion to how much difficulty the adoptive parents might have with their own sexuality and aggression, the child might become both "our" good child and "their" bad child. The child, inevitably perceiving these parental representations of herself, will incorporate them into the self-representation, and then is likely to repeatedly test the commitment of the adoptive parents, increasing demands for acceptance by engaging in behavior that becomes more and more unacceptable to them. The child can end up provoking exactly the outcome that is feared.

THE CASE OF JACQUELINE

In the case of Jacqueline, we certainly see an example of the vivid power of a child's fantasy life, and the special use of a favorite fantasy to consolidate all sorts of issues in the intrapsychic experience of being adopted, much as "family romances" (Freud 1908) are utilized by all children in navigating the conflicts of the oedipal period. Whatever else one may think of them, the Disney adaptations of classics such as *Peter Pan* provide colorful material for the weaving of children's own private tapestries. The technicolor images last so well, and reach so deep, that I would question whether many of us here can sit through them with our children with a dry eye, and those of us who grew up with these stories, not with *Sesame Street* or *Star Wars*, may remember as I do playing out with cousins and neighbors such scenes as Peter, Wendy, and the Red Indians.

In her play sessions with her analyst, Jacqueline took on

aspects of Wendy, Peter, and Nana, while contending dramatically with the forces represented by Tinker Bell and Captain Hook. The story has much to do with whether one succumbs to the appeal of Never Never Land, a frozen state of narcissistic invulnerability, grandiosity, and denial of not only adult authority but also the realities of the world, or whether one somehow moves ahead in development. Like a Peter Pan, Jacqueline came to analysis with every indication of being stuck in a destructive cycle of unhappiness and rage with the world her adoptive parents tried to offer her. Dr. Silverman, however, seems to have connected with the glimpse of Wendy, ambivalent about Never Never Land, that he saw in Jacqueline's own unhappiness and her willingness to reach out to him, despite all her ferocious guardedness.

In a therapeutic process that I think is truly lovely, because love was at the core of it, Dr. Silverman functioned as only a child analyst is trained to do, allowing himself to be used as a role-playing actor in the child's fantasies while maintaining an active objective position as a real object. This is a complex set of functions, and in itself answers to a large extent what was therapeutic.

Accepting the child's direction in play simultaneously manifests a creatively regressive capacity to share in a child's position of passivity and submissiveness, and allows for a deep rapport of communication between the two. Also, just as one may or may not have an aptitude for being absorbed in the communication of a piece of music, or a work of art, the child analyst exemplified here can attune very closely to what cannot be verbally articulated by a young child.

Crucial for the formation of an analytic situation and process with a child of this age was Dr. Silverman's awareness that he would have to tolerate the narcissistic pain of Jacqueline's affectless and cold manipulation and rejections of him. Only by doing so, and verbalizing to her "I can understand" and "I can wait," could he provide her the sense of relative safety that she would need. Only with that demonstration of maturity and endurance on his part could she proceed to open up to him in her story. With it being a process, and her being a child with massive reasons to doubt the certainty of her object world, this capacity for empathetic safety would have to be tested again and again.

Very interesting discoveries were made, unique to this child, but relevant to us all. The preverbal fairy Tinker Bell in Jacqueline's version of the story stands as a poignant figure for anyone feeling victimized by rejection. Jacqueline split herself apart defensively as an uncaring "bad mother" who would coldly allow Tinker Bell to pine away and die, "unknowing" until experiencing it via the analyst's sensitivity that she would thus allow her own heart to freeze and crack. When Dr. Silverman said to her, "Maybe fairies are part human," I think he was in effect interpreting "Maybe Tinker Bell is a part of you." However, Tinker Bell was pining away for Peter, who was always off protecting the "lost boys," fighting Red Indians, and winning hearts of human girls. I wonder if this might also have expressed the girl's need for her *fathers*, both the one who could never be there for her and the adoptive father whom we sense also as being far way at his work and perhaps not fully there for her when at home either. We should not assume that all the hurt and rage is derived from motherlessness, and I am not referring only to the father as an oedipal object.

In their dialogue about Peter Pan "caring about nothing," Dr. Silverman and the child were looking both at her stance of defense against narcissistic pain and at her identification with the abandoning birth parents (and perhaps also the too-much-absent adoptive father). We have a whole other dimension, I think, when the focus changes to Captain Hook.

Here perhaps is the level of work in understanding psychopathology that is ordinarily beyond the expectations of most parents, let alone adoptive parents, yet had better not be beyond the expectations and aptitudes of the child therapist.

For children, Captain Hook is one of the more terrifying manifestations of evil, incorporating possessive greed, envy that transgresses all boundaries and is willing to destroy, and relentless pursuit of vengeance. For children, Hook might be seen as an

Ahab, willing to go to the ends of the earth if necessary, and take all with him, for the sake of revenge over loss. A comical inversion of Ahab, who pursues his Moby Dick, the great Leviathan of natural forces of finality woven into the world, Hook cowers in panic at the thought of the crocodile relentlessly pursuing him, the ticking clock of inevitable Time in its jaws. Such a human element as Hook is not beyond resorting to murder out of envy and fear of further loss. And this is the key: it is, nonetheless, a human element, not to be denied as potential in us all, even in young children. We all learn about death wishes, but it is important not to be too guarded against this level of hate when working with a patient, or, I might add, when counseling adolescents.

Again, we all have been hearing much about "the Dark Side" as the *Star Wars* legends have briefly come back into popular consciousness with the 1999 release of another episode. Dr. Silverman has nicely described a series of moments with Jacqueline when he reacted defensively, or felt "shocked" with her attitudes and impulses. One instance was when Jacqueline's Hook coldly killed his first mate Smee. It is quite a challenge to feel for the unbelievable potential of murderous rage that grows out of abandonment. This is indeed the dark side of human nature.

A MATTER OF HEARTBREAK

Thinking of a tragic poet who wrote about "heartbreak" being at the center of all things, I was moved to ponder: What is heartbreak? It might not only be the pain at work when a child is given up forever to the care of others; it might also be what's felt by those of us who have had a father go off to war, and on return never be fully "home" again. Or it might be like the damage to those who have gone off to war with golden promises, let loose to be killing machines, and then feel that they have lost a part of themselves forever. It may be like the effect on those who have had a mother cry in depressed agitation that she "never wanted children anyway."

Such "heartbreak" on the part of a child often emerges in the setting of a divorce. A 10-year-old boy I have in analysis, full of spunky curiosity and intelligence and moments of tender affection, returns from visits with his father, a father who is always busy with work and commitments to others, virtually mute with frustration and anger that he needs to deny in order to keep the father idealized, even weeping with the complaint of what a horrible "headache" he has. Another 10-year-old, a dark-skinned Puerto Rican boy adopted by white parents along with two other children of different races, who is terribly destructive at home when in a rage, would bite or spit at me in a labile moment, as if to spit into the face of his inner abandonment. "I'm dead," he has said at times, or "I suck," if a checkers move goes wrong for him. Lately he asks, "Am I a nigger?"

What terrible cavity of heart is it that allows two adolescents to giggle with each other while loading their automatic weapons to go out and blow away their world? Do we find heartbreak in the motives of those who are always searching, as if for some lost "other"? Is this feeling like that of refugees and exiles, those banished from their homelands? After all, Elie Wiesel (1985) has said, "Exile is total. It envelops all endeavors, all explorations, all illusions, all hopes, all triumphs, and this means that whatever we do is never complete" (p. 27). Is this heartache not like the grief we feel at the death of a parent, or a spouse, or a child?

BACK TO THE CLINICAL MATERIAL

I think it is at those moments when her analyst responded with constancy and willingness to empathize with (or, at least tolerate) the hatred and destructiveness expressed in Jacqueline's fantasies and behavior, that their therapeutic bond that could have easily unraveled, was maintained. When Jacqueline's adoptive parents witnessed her bite the button off Dr. Silverman's sleeve they were "in awe," and clearly not as prepared as he was to accept this "crocodile" behavior in their child. One must observe that among the obstacles for a happy-enough adoption would be not just the idealization of the baby child, which is common to all parents, but the possible overidealization of their own motives, and their own civilized selves in contrast to the more instinctualized "others" who gave up the child. "How could you do that!?" cried even the child analyst in reaction to this child's shredding the valentine's heart she had worked on for him for weeks. "You broke my heart!," he told her. But this time, the constancy of the line of connection was initiated by Jacqueline, when she called him on the telephone after walking out. Though getting even by breaking another's heart is undeniably important, I think she was also correct in insisting it was not; the destructive gesture may not have meant as much as the fact that she preserved her attachment and was willing to talk. This is confirmed by the later material regarding her sharing the mirror space with her analyst.

It would only be speculation, even for the analyst, to guess what reasons compelled the adoptive parents to end Jacqueline's analysis. But I do suppose that a comfortable enough grasp of what was involved in this treatment on its most effectual level might be beyond the tolerance of most parents. Part of the success of the treatment as reported, though, and a substantial consolation, is that this child appeared to have learned that there was the possibility in the world for her experiences of hurt and rage to be understood, accepted, and countered with love. We should be hopeful that when she is caught up in the whirlpool of those forces again, she will remember that she knows how to reach out rather than destroy.

Ultimately, in the same world of stars or whatever it is "up there" that visits upon us death and loss, great white whales, wily sharks, dangerous crocodiles, and gone-away parents, we are fortunate indeed to somehow come up with the likes of a Martin Silverman, or a Selma Kramer, or a Margaret Mahler.

REFERENCES

Brinich, P. M. (1980). Some potential effects of adoption upon self and object representations. *Psychoanalytic Study of the Child* 35:107–135. New Haven, CT: Yale
University Press.

Freud, S. (1908). Family romances. *Standard Edition* 9:235–244.

Peller, L. (1961). About "telling the child" of his adoption. *Bulletin of the Philadelphia
Association for Psychoanalysis* 11:145–154, 1961.

Wieder, H. (1977a). On being told of adoption. *Psychoanalytic Quarterly* 46:1–22.

——— (1977b). The family romance fantasies of adopted children. *Psychoanalytic
Quarterly* 46:185–200.

Wiesel, E. (1985). We are all witnesses. *Parabola* 10(2):26–33.

10

TOWARD OPTIMIZING THE ADOPTED CHILD'S DEVELOPMENT

Concluding Reflections

Robert C. Prall, M.D.
and Henri Parens, M.D.

This book has discussed the complex issues, difficulties, and rewards adoption presents for the adopted child and the adopting parents. The chapters presented by the three key speakers of this symposium add importantly to our understanding of these issues. The chapters by Drs. Carlotta Miles and Marshall Schechter elucidate crucial aspects of the adoption experience and some of the vicissitudes of adoptive parent–child interaction. The chapter by Dr. Martin Silverman documents the degree of injury a mishandled adoption process may cause. He also demonstrates the capability of psychoanalysis to get to the roots of the injury and gradually bring about healing.

TOWARD OPTIMIZING TRANSRACIAL ADOPTION

It is important to consider the problems specific to adoptions across racial, ethnic, and cultural lines, as presented by Dr. Miles, an African-American psychiatrist and psychoanalyst who for years has committed herself to addressing the challenges that come with transracial adoptions. Adoption adds unique complexity to a child's attachments, development, and adaptation, and to a parent's attachment and the work of parenting. The parameter of adoption across racial, ethnic, or cultural lines is an additional complexity. Americans who are seriously motivated to be parents are pushing aside racial identity formation factors for the sake of having one child or more, for the sake of making a family. Psychotherapists can help facilitate this process for both adopted child and parent.

Miles discusses the crucial identity formation factors that must be recognized and dealt with constructively in order to secure for the child the best possible adaptation to our racially mixed society. Pretending that color differences do not exist, being benevolently "color-blind," or ignoring primary identity formation factors that reside in the parent–child relationship does not facilitate the child's efforts to assimilate glaringly visible differences between him- or herself and the primary love objects. In addition, it burdens rather than facilitates identity formation, and it does not help the child adapt socially. We think that Miles's focus on this problem is especially useful, given that identity formation in the child adopted into an interracial family setting is more challenging for the child than it is in same-race adoptions.

At the American Academy of Child Psychiatry (AACP) conference in Bottle Hollow, Utah, representatives of many Native-American cultures from throughout the country met with members of the academy and representatives from various agencies involved in work with Native Americans (AACP 1977). One major point of agreement was that the then-common practice of cross-cultural adoption of Native-American children by white families was detrimental to the children's ability to develop a sense of their cultural identity. As with the process described by Miles regarding other transcultural adoptions, these children suffered similar psychological problems. The difficulties were especially widespread during their adolescence.

The conference stressed the fallacy of the assumption that

governed the previous practice of taking Native-American children from their society and tribes and placing them in boarding schools to optimize their development and acculturation, which led to problems in development. Among the recommendations of the conference were to encourage the placement of such children with Native-American families, if possible of the same tribe or in a nearby tribe; and to develop resources for training of Native-American personnel to work with families in distress and Native-American foster and adoptive families. The conference emphasized the importance of their cultural heritage for Native-American children and made far-reaching recommendations in support of that position.

The conference highlighted the fact that the tribal justice systems were superior to the local county systems in handling the problems caused by Native-American family breakups and in placing children at risk or emotionally disturbed. The AACP had issued in January 1975 a policy statement urging careful consideration in placing Native-American children, and had recommended that placements be the responsibility of the tribal government rather than federal, state, or local agencies (AACP 1975).

Miles draws attention to the painful problems created by prejudice that adoptive parents face in adopting an other-race child. Prejudice is an unavoidable part of people's identity formation. As Parens (1997a) reported,

> It is essential in order to be a member of, and to maintain the specific distinctiveness of a family, community, society, that children identify with the objects in their families, communities, societies. . . . But paradoxically, the attachments and identifications that make for healthy identities are part of the process that brings with it stranger anxiety and facilitate rejection of the different, . . . [which] plays a key role in the predisposition to prejudice [in each of us]. [pp. 138–139]

Many childless couples who want to have children are resistant to adoption. The reasons vary and are addressed in the adoption literature. Miles reports that American black men are "extremely resistant to adopting another man's child," and discusses the possible reasons for this. Miles also discusses the prejudicial stereotyping of adoptable children on the basis of racial and ethnic categorizations.

Many parents who have adopted other-race children are aware of some of the challenges differing racial traits bring with them and are able to deal with them constructively. Difficulties encountered with rearing these children often come not from transracial factors, but from the early childhood traumatizations that many adopted children were subjected to.

Miles informs us that there has been increasing recognition of key problems that come with transracial adoptions, and she tells us how the Barker Foundation deals with these problems. It is regrettable but not surprising that well-intentioned adoptive parents are likely to encounter hardships in confronting these challenges. The parents' willingness to help the child identify with his or her own race entails investing emotionally at a primary-object level (Parens et al. 1997) cathecting with love unreservedly, and letting the child's core identity be different from the parents'. It is essential that we let our children decide what foods they like, who their friends are, what they want to be, who they want to marry, and so on. But this does not apply as freely to letting our children be themselves at the basic core level of who we are as selves and as members of a family and a society. This challenges too disruptively parents' own sense of identity and community. This is why we see parents reject their children when they change their religion, for instance. Complex, long-term processes form our self-image, our sense of self, and our primary-level valuation of objects (Freud 1939 [1940]). For other-race adoptive parents these processes require expansion or revision. Some parents can do this, but others may falter, experience anxiety, or feel hostility toward the child, and they need help in meeting these challenges.

It is critical, as Miles points out, for adoptive parents to know that the adopted child, in the process of attachment, will identify with all aspects of the parenting objects, including the color of their skin. The black child constructs a self-image of a white-skinned child. What, then, goes through the child's mind when he looks in the mirror and sees his appearance is not the same as his earliest internal self-concept? What goes on in the 15-month-old's mind when he is now surrounded by an adoptive family that speaks a language he never heard before? We believe that the identification process begins long before latency; it begins from about the fourth and fifth months of extrauterine life. We have seen remarkable identifications with Mother's caregiving, for good and bad, in children during the early part of the second year of life (Parens and Pollock 1979).

Our clinical experience leads us to the same starkly painful conclusion to which Miles has come, namely that "the key question of every adoptee is, 'Why did she give me away?'" Working with adopted children has given us the same impression of this narcissistic wound, which is highly resistant to healing and often leads to a difficult-to-analyze sense of entitlement that we encounter in harshly traumatized individuals.

Miles recommends ways of helping transracial adoptive parents. We believe her recommendations are valid for the prevention of the potentially painful problems other-race adoptive children are unwittingly set up to experience.

ON BIOGENETIC DETERMINANTS OF ATTACHMENT AND THEIR ROLE IN ADOPTION

Dr. Schechter's major thesis is one that we believe has been insufficiently recognized, especially by psychotherapists. Focusing his lens on what determines the crucial process of attachment (Bowlby 1958, 1969, Spitz 1946a, 1965), Schechter draws attention to the roles biogenetic determinants and intrauterine events can play in adoptive parent–child interaction and the evolving of their reciprocal attachment. Schechter points to some of these influences on organizing and shaping early-life character traits already discernible from birth on.

Schechter has worked with and studied adopted children and their parents since the start of his clinical practice fifty years ago. He enjoins us to be aware of those parent–child emotional dialogue derailments that may not derive purely from failures in emotionally determined dynamics of their interaction, such as maternal/paternal insufficiently empathic or excessively anxious reactivity. He also enjoins us to consider biogenetically driven differences in dispositions and reactivities between child and parent, for example, a quick-reactor infant with a slow-reactor mother, that are likely to lead secondarily to psychodynamic interactional disharmonies. Therapists have taken temperament dispositions and mother–child character trait dissimilarities into consideration, but not enough weight has been given to these biogenetic co-determiners.

The studies and findings Schechter presents illuminate specific areas we need to attend to in our work with adoptive parent–child pairs. He is right to assert that the factors in question are not trivial ones, as they substantially affect characteristic interactional patterns and co-determine even more complex, emotionally weighty aspects of parent–child interaction influencing factors such as talents, humor, interests, and worldviews. Biogenetic determination is readily recognized when it comes to physical traits such as the color of hair and eyes, shapes of noses, and height, but it is less recognized when it comes to psychological traits. We think it is enormously important to look for such possible sources of problem when we try to understand the nature of parent–child emotional dialogue derailments and how to help adoptive parents deal with them by optimizing parenting strategies.

In the field of child development it is well known that incompatibilities in even biological mother and child pairs can lead to serious interactional disharmonies that cause derailment of their evolving emotional dialogue. Such derailment is most often ascribed to either variability in mother–child character traits—with insufficient emphasis on their biogenetic determinants—or to difficulties in the mother, most commonly considered of a pathologic nature, or in the infant, most commonly considered to be due to an inborn development defect or of a temperature nature.

Schechter's work suggests that we might need to give more consideration to how derailments in adoptive parent–child relationships may result not simply from pathology in the mother but from biogenetically determined incompatibilities. In biological mother–child pairs, 50 percent of their gene pool is the same. This still allows for a large margin of possible incompatibilities between them.

As Schechter asserts, the problems are especially multiplied in adoptive mother–child pairs. Here, the gene pool is completely different. Compatibilities are as accidental as incompatibilities. This seems to be particularly pertinent to the attachment process and to separation-individuation, and such biogenetically determined parent–child incompatibilities may plague both child and parent for many years. Being alert to this source of incompatibility equips us better as psychodynamic clinicians to work more effectively with adoptive parents.

Many parents are quick to blame themselves or blame the adopted child, on emotional grounds, for failures in attachment, problems in the child–parent relationship, or for less than optimal development of the child. But these parent–child incompatibilities, whatever their degree, do not present insurmountable obstacles to the formation of a constructive parent–child dialogue. Clinicians must not only examine that derailing emotional dialogue but also develop task-specific strategies for parents who have adopted a child with significantly different inborn dispositions and reactivity patterns. Our experiences with parents document the many ways in which we can help them see and understand how the discrepancies in dispositions and reactivities between themselves and their young children lead to stresses between them and undermine the love the adoptive parents bring to the child. Explanation of such biogenetic or intrauterine determining factors and examples help parents develop more optimal interactional strategies.

The work of Mahler and colleagues (1975), Parens (1972), and Parens and colleagues (1974) both confirm and further elaborate the original work of Spitz and Bowlby on attachment. The formation of close intrapsychic bonds, as Schechter speaks of it, is a progressive process that begins as early as 6 to 12 weeks of age and becomes sufficiently organized into specific and stable attachments from 5 months of age on. There is ample evidence of a progressive attachment process that is manifested in social smiling responses, separation anxiety, stranger anxiety, and reunion reactions—the four indices of attachment (Parens 1972) that appear well before 6 months of age. Nor is it our understanding that Bowlby assumed that infants are initially capable of forming only one attachment, as Schechter suggests. Observational evidence shows that, on the part of the infant, the attachment process can be put into motion and develop substantially with several objects, such as mother, father, and even siblings. The larger determinant of this attachment comes from the emotional availability of, and the emotional investment made in the infant by, the parents.

TRAUMATIZING ADOPTION MAY LEAD TO RESISTANCE AND FAILURE IN ATTACHMENT

How impressed we were by Dr. Martin Silverman's sensitive and masterful psychoanalytic treatment of Jacqueline. His treatment report lays out the harsh consequence to this then 4-year-old child who, due to accidental circumstances, such as the efforts by the adoption agency and state regulations to be protective of those concerned, suffered serious impediment to her attachment to her adoptive parents. Unable to override their own anxieties and inhibitions, the adoptive parents unknowingly contributed to Jacqueline's resistance to attachment.

Silverman describes the normal vicissitudes wrought by ambivalence in all parent–child relationships. All normal children get angry, feel hostile toward, and even hate the parents they love; similarly, normal parents get angry, feel hostile toward, and at moments may even hate their children. Parens (1999) has conceptualized processes that secure unconditional love in normal parents, especially in mothers, toward their biological children, which gives cogency to Silverman's discussion of this issue.

Clinicians must be aware of the vulnerability to attachment in adoptive situations, and must help adoptive parents make secure for the adopted child the relatedness that will withstand interludes of hostility, episodes of rage, and even transient hate. Parents who understand the importance of these matters are much more likely to be effective than parents who are not so informed (Parens 1993, Parens et al. 1994, 1997). Silverman helped Jacqueline's mother understand the vicissitudes of attachment and be more secure, less guilty, and more positive in her interactions with Jacqueline.

Silverman's detailing of the treatment demonstrates his skills in empathic openness, patience, sensitivity, and child analytic play technique. His allowing Jacqueline to choose the thematic metaphor gave her the reins to direct the action of their experience in her transference. Silverman immersed himself skillfully and sensitively in the child's character assignments, which most likely led to the success of the unfolding treatment.

We know child analysis is powerful, but Silverman asks some meaningful questions: (1) What was therapeutic about the process? (2) What was the role of his being willing to share her pain and suffering? (3) What happened when he told her she had broken his heart? (4) What is the key element in the process of analytic cure?

Questions 1 and 4 are best answered by assuming that multiple factors led to the successful outcome: putting into words; drawing connections; making the painful affects and thoughts bearable by virtue of his auxiliary-ego function of containment and holding while she suffered; reliving what she had to suppress in order to stay sufficiently integrated, so that now, bit by bit, she could use the therapist as transference object to experience the meaningful engagement in her relationship with him; and taking many defensive steps to make her experience bearable.

In response to question 2, we would say that to make her suffering gradually bearable for her he had to let himself empathically feel what it was she suffered. But we think he had to go a step further than just putting the experience into words of just empathizing. In his "benign transference enactment" (Parens 1997b), participating in her directed enactment of *Peter Pan* and her transference assignments, Silverman showed Jacqueline that he perceived and sympathized with her pain, her initially merciless rage, and her anguish. In such benign transference enactment, the analyst participates in the analytic play, putting himself in the place of the child in the given transference moment, letting himself feel, as the child might feel, a transient "near-identification," which can mirror and reflect to the child the pain the child cannot at that moment let herself feel and deal with. In this mirroring, Jacqueline's identification with the aggressor served her well, because her analyst could enact with genuine feeling the part of the despairing heartbroken Tinker Bell as well as the raging but tortured captain Hook.

Silverman was able to go so far as to exclaim in momentary genuine pain in this benign transference enactment that in tearing up the valentine card she had made for him, she had broken his heart, not only as Peter repeatedly did to Tinker Bell, but as had in fact happened to her in her early life object loss. Jacqueline did not engage in attachment with her adoptive parents, which perpetuated the feeling of loss and heartbreak. Note that Silverman did not take the heartbreak experience back to the metaphoric Tinker Bell. He took it back directly into her transference, where he, the transference object, felt the awful pain of heartbreak. Some analysts speak of this as pertaining to the transference–countertransference sphere of analytic experience. But the term *countertransference* has come to be used so broadly as to have lost specific meaning. We prefer to speak of this as lending oneself as transference object to engage the patient from within the patient's transference rather than from outside. We usually position ourselves outside the transference to make running commentaries, confrontations, and interpretations, as Mahler suggested. We do not subscribe to therapists' disclosing their countertransference experiences to the patient, using "countertransference" in its original definition of a neurotic, usually unconscious, reaction within the analyst activated by the patient's transference.

Silverman was skillful in another sector of child analytic work. Mahler taught the importance of recognizing nonverbal cues as the child reacts to our commentaries, confrontations, and interpretations (Kramer and Prall 1971). She spoke of a range of responses she called green-, yellow-, or red-light responses. She emphasized that by carefully observing the child's facial expressions and body language, one could monitor the child's reactions to our interventions. These reactions direct the next step we take. In this, Silverman was astute. Early in Jacqueline's analysis, the many "red-light" responses he got to his interventions, such as when she would not let him finish a statement, informed him of the child's resistances, and he paced his interventions in a manner that made possible the child's progressively becoming able to tolerate his efforts to gently push the line of these resistances. In Mahler's sense, it may be that Jacqueline wished for and feared symbiotic reengulfment, and that she had to defend against this by pulling away from her analyst lest she become aware of these unconscious wishes.

From Jacqueline's not being able to tolerate his commentaries of what Silverman saw going on, he found his way to generalizing about children's reactions to losing someone to whom they were attached. She gave him a "sharp, ambiguous look," but she did not hide under the table as she had been doing. We saw this as well at the point where Silverman felt she could tolerate his pushing her resistance by saying that he was sympathetic to Tinker Bell's starving to death, that Tinker Bell had feelings, too. "So do you!" she retorted, a "yellow-light" response.

And how rightly he read her yellow-light signs again, when he ventured to propose that Tinker Bell, on the point of almost dying, could perhaps be allowed to live. Jacqueline took an interactive step toward him: "How could we do that?" she asked. For the first time, she had used the pronoun *we*. Did this not document Silverman's empathic perception that, with due caution, she was ready to let him proceed as he had? She could now allow her transfer object to mean more to her; she could now work with her analyst toward reducing her psychic isolation and her emotional starvation for object love. When Jacqueline agreed to allow Wendy (Silverman) to minister to and nurse Tinker Bell (Jacqueline) back to health, she gave clear evidence of accepting his helping her to better health. When he proposed that "maybe fairies are part human," her response was a yellow light—she looked "thoughtful" rather than "sharp and ambiguous" or otherwise rejecting of his comment.

Jacqueline's permitting Silverman to proceed with due yellow-light caution gradually yielded green-light responses. For instance, in the waiting room, she became angry with her analyst when, on the point of going on a vacation to Disney World, she experienced the separation as if it was he, the transference object, who was abandoning her. And there was confirmation of his reading of her when, startled by her biting a button off his sleeve, he interpreted that he thought she wanted to eat him up to have him inside her; she confirmed this with, "Then you can never leave me." And there were other green lights, perhaps none more touching than when she was stroking the breast of the naked statue, and, having "wolfed down" the tangerine, she stroked its rind. Appropriately tentatively Silverman said, "You know what I think? [He did not impose his thought on her, he asked her to think about it.] I think you want me to grow breasts and become a Mommy for you." Her exclamation, "Could you!" vehemently confirmed his timely and insightful interpretation of her fantasy. Such a progression from intolerance of virtually any interpretation to confirming responsiveness tells us of the skill of the analyst in understanding his patient's resistances and his pacing and dosing his interventions to achieve the child's tolerance for such depth interpretation.

In addition to these skills, Silverman's knowledge of development, structure formations, and evolving self and object relatedness served him well and contributed to what made the analysis work. He knew, for instance, of Mahler's (and other analysts') pointing out that failures of object constancy derive from failures in early attachment and separation-individuation, and that such failures make for serious problems in the formation of healthy relationships. He understood that Jacqueline's wish to have his picture with her on her trip to Disney World was suggestive of a weakness in object constancy. And so was Jacqueline's phone call 45 minutes after she had exploded in his office. Enraged with him for his insisting on having to stop their session when she resisted leaving, just as she had completed the valentine card she made for him, she tore it into pieces and stalked out. We think Silverman is right that she called to reconstruct or to reattach the pieces of his image in her mind, which she had ripped to pieces along with the valentine card destined for him; how supportive it is of Silverman's pointing to the large degree of difficulty ambivalence can cause adoptive-mother–rearer children, difficulty not only for the parents but perhaps even more so for the adopted child. And, indeed, ambivalence is a large contributor to undermining the development of object constancy.

The 46-year-old patient Prall (1997) described in his presentation at the 27th annual Mahler symposium on the seasons of life also showed such evidence of insufficiently developed object constancy. She, too, needed a photograph and even a tape recording of Prall's voice to have with her during their first of a number of vacation-imposed separations. From this, she progressed in the consolidation of the internal image she held of him by calling his office to hear his voice on the tape. Prall reconstructed her psychopathology to having its roots in her rapprochement subphase when her brother was born, in consequence of which she felt acutely abandoned by her depressed mother who seemed to be in a "glass box." Parens, too, has been photographed by patients and called hours after sessions to be asked, in fact by an adopted child, "What are you doing?" "What did you eat for dinner?" or still in a

session, "What are you gonna eat tonight?"—all in the service of
intrapsychic object–image stabilization.

A LONG-RECOGNIZED BUT
UNFINISHED TASK LIES BEFORE US

Important as the questions of analysis are to us, highly important as
well as Dr. Silverman's bringing into clarity the depth of Jacqueline's traumatization, a traumatization unwittingly brought about
by burdensome government-sponsored "protective" strategies imposed on her as well as on her adoptive parents. Such unintended
injury done to very young children can have a scarring impact on
them. In accord with the state regulations in force where she was
born, Jacqueline was first placed for six months in a foster home
with an older, affectionately warm, attentive woman to whom she
attached well. Reportedly, she was happy and thriving. At the age
of 6 months, at the peak of the first consolidation of this attachment, during her symbiotic phase, she was taken from this already
well-organizing and establishing relationship for adoption. In spite
of the good intentions of this adoptive could, Jacqueline experienced acutely the loss of her first libidinal (attachment) object. She
cried pitifully, would neither eat nor sleep, howled, and could not
attach to her adoptive mother (see Bowlby 1960, 1969, Spitz
1946b, 1965).

Compounding the ill-timed adoption—about three months
too late to make an object shift before attachment sufficiently
organizes and cements—the adopting couple lived under constant
fear that the child might be taken from them. (The adoption agency
was mandated by state law to make periodic visits to determine
whether the child was adjusting well. Not knowing the predict-
ability or normalcy of Jacqueline's distressing loss reaction, it is
highly understandable that the adoptive parents, and even the
agency worker, would have assumed that the adoption was not
proceeding well. Under state law, the adoption could not be

finalized until after one year.) This fear caused a substantial inhibition in the adoptive mother's—and possibly also the father's—ability to fully embrace Jacqueline emotionally. Spitz (1960) found that in such first-year object losses, the infant could be protected from a profound distress reaction by providing a substitute object with positively caring and nurturing characteristics similar to those of the lost object. The threat of the child's being taken from them prevents many well-motivated parents from providing the needed degree of emotional availability that makes positive and nurturing-enough caregiving possible (Mahler et al. 1975). Some years ago, in a somewhat similar case with a perhaps more vulnerable child, the outcome was even more drastic than it was for Jacqueline (Parens 1972).

Complicating matters yet further was the fact that Jacqueline's adoptive mother revealed that because of a tubercular lesion in her breast, and fearing she might infect her daughter, she did not hold her child during the first 6 months of their life together. Misinformed, the mother added to what the state and the adoption agency had inflicted on the vulnerable emotional component of the adoption process.

This case highlights the fact that well-intentioned, government-imposed protective measures have on many occasions been clinically documented to interfere with adoptive parents' opening themselves fully emotionally to attaching to and to receiving unreservedly the young child's thrusts into attachment. Over the years, we have encountered other unwitting interferences perpetrated by misguided government guidelines for dealing with adoptions.

Goldstein and colleagues (1973) decried the harm done to children by society and by well-intentioned government institutions. Goldstein and colleagues (1996) described the tragic case of Baby Richard, whose adoption was delayed and eventually derailed by the courts until he was nearly 3½ years old. Richard was given up at birth by his unmarried mother without the consent of the absent father. The father later reappeared and married the mother.

They then sued for custody of their biological child. Local and appellate courts denied their petition. Appeal was made to the Supreme Court. Unaware of the probable harm it would cause, and pushing aside the rights of the young child, the Supreme Court reversed the lower court's decision and awarded custody of Richard to the biological parents, who had never touched or even seen the child. The gratifying relationship Richard had established with his adoptive parents was abruptly terminated without even minimal preparation for all concerned.

The 1969 Revised Uniform Adoption Act mandated a 6-month waiting period before adoption can be finalized. In 1996, Goldstein and colleagues argued against this legislation, stating, "Adoption in the early weeks of an infant's life enhances the chance for the adoptive parents and child to develop a psychological parent–child relationship" (p. 13). We agree with the authors that the enormous pain and scarring perpetrated on Jacqueline and Baby Richard could have been avoided if the adoption process had been accelerated and more quickly finalized. Psychoanalytic and attachment researchers and theorists have documented the importance the attachment process holds for the child's development and lifelong well-being. They assert that in the normal child the process of attachment begins from birth and achieves its first stability at about 5 to 7 months, during the symbiotic mutually need-fulfilling mother–child relationship. This crucial process becomes patterned in the brain and psyche over the span of the first three years of life. When this process is achieved with good enough quality, we can say that the child's attachments to parental figures and later to positive authority figures, peers, mate, and offspring will be good enough. Delays in the smooth progression of this process, or poorly substituted and unprepared interruptions of it, can have drastic consequences. Therefore, acceleration of the adoption process is necessary and its disruptions must be minimized. In Jacqueline, we saw so lucidly and in depth the consequences of such delay, interruption, and inhibition of emotional availability on the part of the adoptive mother—in large part out of anxiety that the child would be taken away from her. Without the intensive treatment Dr. Silverman was able to carry out with Jacqueline, we are convinced that her traumatization would have had lifelong highly destructive consequences. Her distress might well have been prevented by prompt and permanent adoption. The thorough evaluation of the adoptive parents must occur before the adoption wheels are set in motion, not after.

More recent attempts to improve adoption practices are being made. In one example, the Pennsylvania legislature, at the recommendation of the State Government Commission on Adoption, Senate Resolution 72 (1995) was adopted on November 25, 1996. It established an advisory committee to study and make recommendations on adoption regulations for Pennsylvania. A report is expected early in the year 2000.

Closely linked to the adoption question is the foster-care question. In talking about foster-home placements, Goldstein and colleagues (1996) made clear the clinically substantiated fact that long-term positive foster placement, especially of young children, invariably leads to the formation of a close reciprocal attachment between child and foster parent. They emphasized the profound traumatic effects that can follow from interruptions of such relationships. This was the case for Jacqueline. On the one hand, Goldstein and colleagues advocate that foster placement should be as brief as reasonably possible. On the other hand, where long-term placement leads to positive attachments, disruption of such attachment must be done only when absolutely necessary, and preparation for separation and continuation of visitation should be strongly encouraged. Continuation of visitation with positively invested former foster parents can contribute most positively to the success of an adoption. In line with efforts to improve adoption legislative regulations, a 1992 New York statute (New York Social Service Law 374, 1-a, 1992) gives preference to foster parents in consideration for adoption of a child who has been in their custody for more than twelve months.

Wherever possible, it is among our responsibilities to inform the public as well as government agencies and legislators of what we have learned from the clinical situation and from psychological research on attachment, so that we can, as Freud (1933) hoped we would, apply these findings to the rearing of the next generation.

Little Jacqueline teaches us yet one more meaningful thing. She brings to mind Stanley Cath's (1997) presentation at the 27th annual Mahler symposium. He talked about the reciprocal importance to each other of grandchild and grandparents. We heard of Jacqueline's valuing most positively her relationship with her maternal grandmother, who lived far away and who no doubt reminded her of the warm older foster mother of her first 6 months.

Was it altogether inadvertent that in Dr. Silverman's office Jacqueline called someone at random in Hawaii? In wondering this, we do not at all question Silverman's musing with Jacqueline as to whether in having reached a woman so far away Jacqueline might not have been "looking for [her] first mother," as he said to her. In adoption situations, adoptive grandparents may supply to the child an additional source of love and feeling valued. Some yearning-to-be grandparents are troubled by their own grown children's inability to conceive. They may experience narcissistic injury at not having blood grandchildren to continue their fantasied wished-for blood-line–carried immortality (Cath 1997, Cath et al. 1982).

One of the authors is a grandfather and great-grandfather who values deeply his relationships with his grandchildren and great-grandchildren, and who had the good fortune to have known not only his own grandparents but also two great-grandmothers; he thus knew seven generations of his family. He has developed a foster grandparents program at his church in which he matches families of young children who have no grandparents with older people who have no grandchildren or whose grandchildren live far away. The outcome has been rewarding. One successful example is that of the family of a young colleague, Bill, who has two young children, a 3-year-old girl and a 1-year-old boy, and to whom an awful tragedy occurred. Prior to that event, through activity in the church, this young family had been paired with an older couple in

Prall's foster grandparents program. The tragedy occurred when the family was driving home from a trip. Bill was asleep in the back of the van and the children were securely fastened in their car seats. The mother, who was driving, somehow ran off the road, the van rolled over, and she was killed instantly. The children were only slightly hurt but their father was seriously injured, sustaining fractures of his pelvis and both legs, and other injuries. The officers on the scene could find no relatives to contact. However, they did find in the mother's purse the name and telephone number of their foster grandparents, who promptly came to care for the children. Both foster grandparents were enormously helpful while Bill was in the hospital and then in rehabilitation, and they continued after he came home. Their relationship continues, and is most rewarding to all of them.

Erikson (1959), in his productive epigenetic model of the life cycle, said of the last stage of life that the beginning deserves and needs the end and the end deserves and needs the beginning. In those families where there are positive ties between the generations, the elderly and the children are most fortunate. Those elderly who are not in such families are likely to suffer loneliness and despair.

Prall's work leads to the proposition that adoption agencies and workers ought to be more aware of and weigh the involvement of grandparents in the adoption process, and, where the quality of the involvement is positive, to encourage the participation in adoptive family life of grandparents in the rearing of the adoptive children.

REFERENCES

American Academy of Child Psychiatry. (1975). *Policy Statement: The Placement of American Indian Children: the Need for Change.* Washington, DC: AACP.
———— (1977). *Supportive Care, Custody, Placement and Adoption of American Indian Children.* Washington, DC: AACP.

Bowlby, J. (1958). The nature of the child's attachment to his mother. *International Journal of Psycho-Analysis* 39:350–373.

——— (1960). Grief and mourning in infancy and early childhood. *Psychoanalytic Study of the Child* 15:9–52. New York: International Universities Press.

——— (1969). *Attachment and Loss*, Vol. 1: *Attachment*. New York: Basic Books.

Cath, S. (1997). Loss and restitution in late life. In *The Seasons of Life*, ed. S. Akhtar and S. Kramer, pp. 127–156. Northvale, NJ: Jason Aronson.

Cath S., Gurwitt, A. R., and Ross, J. M. (1982). *Father and Child: Developmental and Clinical Perspectives*. Boston: Little, Brown.

Erikson, E. H. (1959). *Identity and the Life Cycle*. Psychological Issues, monograph 1. New York: International Universities Press.

Freud, S. (1933). New introductory lectures on psycho-analysis. *Standard Edition* 22:3–182.

——— (1939[1940]). An outline of psychoanalysis. *Standard Edition* 23:141–207.

Goldstein, J., Freud, A., and Solnit, A. J. (1973). *Beyond the Best Interests of the Child*. New York: Free Press.

Goldstein, J., Solnit, A. J., Goldstein, S., and Freud, A. (1996). *The Best Interests of the Child: The Least Detrimental Alternative*. New York: Free Press.

Kramer, S., and Prall, R. C. (1971). A child psychoanalysis training program. In *Separation-Individuation: Essays in Honor of Margaret S. Mahler*, ed. J. B. McDevitt and C. F. Settlage, pp. 486–498. New York: International Universities Press.

Mahler, M. D., Pine, F., and Bergman, A. (1975). *The Psychological Birth of the Human Infant*. New York: Basic Books.

Parens, H. (1972). Indices of the child's earliest attachment to his mother, applicable in routine pediatric examination. *Pediatrics* 49:600–603.

——— (1993). Toward preventing experience-derived emotional disorders: education for parenting. In *Prevention in Mental Health*, ed. H. Parens and S. Kramer, pp. 121–148. Northvale, NJ: Jason Aronson.

——— (1997a). Toward the prevention of prejudice. In *At the Threshold of the Millennium: Proceedings of the Conference*, ed. M. Lemlij and M. R. Fort, pp. 131–141. Lima, Peru: SIDEA/Prom-Peru.

——— (1997b). *Implications for the clinical situation of reformulations of the psychoanalytic theory of aggression—part 2: implications for the clinical situation.* (Unpublished.)

——— (1999). Notes on mothers' emotional investment in their babies. (In press.)

Parens, H., and Pollock, L. (1979). *The Child's Wish to Have a Baby, Part (Reel) I: Statement of Hypotheses*. Audio-Visual Section, film 4(a). Philadelphia: Eastern Pennsylvania Psychiatric Institute.

Parens, H., Pollock, L., and Prall, R. C. (1974). *Prevention—Early Intervention Mother–Infant Groups*. Audio-Visual Section, film 3. Philadelphia: Eastern Pennsylvania Psychiatric Institute.

Parens, H., Scattergood, E., Duff, S., and Singletary, W. (1997). *Parenting for Emotional Growth: A Curriculum for Students in Grades K Thru 12: A Textbook and Model Lesson Plans*. In-Progress printing by Parenting for Emotional Growth, Philadelphia.

Prall, R. C. (1997). Separation-individuation aspects in later life. In *The Seasons of Life*, ed. S. Akhtar and S. Kramer, pp. 95–125. Northvale, NJ: Jason Aronson.

Spitz, R. (1946a). The smiling response: a contribution to the ontogenesis of social relations. *Genetic Psychology Monographs* 34:57–125.

——— (1946b). Anaclitic depression. *Psychoanalytic Study of the Child* 2:313–342. New York: International Universities Press.

——— (1960). Discussion of J. Bowlby's "Grief and Mourning in Infancy." *Psychoanalytic Study of the Child* 15:85–90. New Haven: Yale University Press.

——— (1965). *The First Year of Life*, with W. G. Cobliner. New York: International Universities Press.

Index